EntréChic ™

The Mega-Guide
to Entrepreneurial
Excéllence

EntréChic ™

The Mega-Guide to Entrepreneurial Excellence

C.E. CRIMMINS

amacom
American Management Association

This book is available at a special dis-
count when ordered in bulk quantities.
For information, contact Special Sales
Department, AMACOM, a division of
American Management Association, 135
West 50th Street, New York, NY 10020.

Library of Congress Cataloging-in-Publication Data

Crimmins, C. E.
    Entrechic : the mega-guide to entrepreneurial
excellence.

    1. Entrepreneur--Anecdotes, facetiae, satire, etc.
I. Title.
PN6231.E65C75   1985   818'.5402   85-47669
ISBN 0-8144-7635-X

Illustrations by Emerson, Wajdowicz Studios, Inc. © 1985

Printing number

10 9 8 7 6 5 4 3 2 1

To the humorous spirit of
David Crimmins, who did it in
the cellar before it was chic.

ACKNOWLEDGMENTS

Mega-thanks are due to: Ron Mallis, who had a gut feeling that entrepreneurs could be funny; Joellen Brown, my one-woman window on the Information Age and brainstorming confidante; R. N. Forman, who risks reading everything I write; and, most especially, Betty Kelly, my personal venture capitalist, who has never failed to provide necessary seed money and encouragement.

I also thank all those who provided access to information and other important services: Brad Wexler, Susan Nagler Perloff, Sarah Babaian, Jackie Siminitus, Susan Erwin, Lisa Yarrow, Scott Wilds, Deborah Gorman, Diedra and Barry Lyngard, Anne Kaier, Sonny C., and Jasper M., who refused to appear in this book.

Finally, a hearty thank you to my in-house legal counsel, Alan Forman, a voice of time-based skepticism in this world of entrepreneurial madness.

Entre-Nous

Many of today's best-known entrepreneurial success stories appear in these pages. Other firms and individuals are figments of the author's imagination. We trust that all armchair entrepreneurs will recognize the difference.

CONTENTS

CONTENTS

1

WELCOME TO THE MEGA-DECADE OF ENTRECHIC

Suddenly they're everywhere. The Cowboy and Cowgirl Capitalists. The Messiahs of the Information Age come to save the American economy. The New Entrepreneurs.

These young and dashing self-employed millionaires of the 1980s hop the continent in their own jets, dance to the wee hours at the nation's trendy night spots, and expose their lean and serious faces on the covers of major newsmagazines.

And then there's you. You're still working in that same boring job. You're still writing memos. You're still paying off the car loan. And you ask yourself, in the words of the infamous Cowardly Lion, "Whatta they got that I ain't got?"

Entrepreneurial chic, that's what. Entrechic for short. It's *the* social skill of the decade, that certain *élan* that precedes astounding success. The cynics will say you either got it or you don't, but don't believe them. Entrepreneurial chic *can* be learned, and we're here to teach it to you.

Entrechic entails far more than business sense. It's a whole way of life that began several years ago when undiscovered geniuses like yourself realized that they *deserved* to become millionaires and overnight celebrities. The ambition to make a financial killing off new concepts has been around since the beginning of time, but it was not until around 1980 A.D. that people honored the process by dubbing it "entrepreneurship." Suddenly, the ruthless and sometimes boring process of setting up new enterprises appeared in a more favorable light. Just as people began talking openly about sex in the 1970s, they began talking candidly about venture capital in the 1980s. No detail appeared too gory to discuss when sex finally came out of the closet, and now that start-ups and capitalization are everyone's fascination, no aspect of the entrepreneurial world appears too sordid for public discussion. If, as Tom Wolfe suggested, the 1970s was the "Me Decade," then the 1980s have added two letters to become the "Mega Decade." And we're already halfway through it. By 1990, everyone in America with any heart will have abandoned his or her entrepreneurial virginity in favor of the pursuit of mega-millions.

Every business day, while you fritter away your time and innate creative abilities in an ordinary job, thousands of people—probably much less intelligent than you—decide to enter the freewheeling entrepreneurial economy by starting up new enterprises. Stop frittering! Don't get left behind in the venture capital sweepstakes. Don't wait until entrepreneurship is so commonplace that even your dog starts a company. Risk it now! Master the nuances of entrechic to become an inner-directed entrepreneur or entrepreneuse who starts up a whole new life. Take the plunge, and gain access to what is the right of every above-average citizen: megabucks, mega-fame, and the mega-leisure to enjoy it all someday soon.

Sure, entrepreneurship also involves some sort of business sense, but we'll get to that less glamorous part later. For now, practice saying the word *entrepreneur* ten times slowly. Remember to pronounce that second "r", just like in *library* or *February*. Can you say it correctly? Do you get that nice little haughty sneer of the lip during the last syllable? Good. Whatever your present occupation, in your heart and at parties you are hereinafter an Entrepreneur. That's your first step toward total entrechicdom.

Now, to understand what you've just become, let's explore the basic historical concept of the entrepreneur.

ENTREPRENEUR VS. SMALL-BUSINESS OWNER

While this country's evolution from the downscale small-business mind set to upscale entrepreneurship is by now pretty much complete, our small-business heritage lingers on in anachronistic names for government agencies, such as the Small Business Administration.

For those who don't remember, "small business" was a concept that embraced anything from a hot dog pushcart to an electronics company with a hundred employees. A small-business owner ran what people quaintly labeled *firms* or *stores* or *outfits.* Fortunately, the term *small-business owner* today is nearly obsolete and strictly *déclassé.* For one thing, no one wants to be called small, least of all inner-directed, ego-healthy types who form their own lucrative ventures. Today even folks with businesses in their garages think mega.

Another term became necessary to aid the self-identities of risk-takers who choose to start their own enterprises. Some popular naming specialists suggested *microbusiness owner,* but the phrase never gained currency. Ultimately, the peculiarly American habit of rehabilitating historic buildings and obsolete words came to the rescue. The coiners of business slang fixed upon the term *entrepreneur,* which had passed into the English language from Old French sometime during the fourteenth century. Its original macho meaning was "one who undertakes—a manager, controller, champion." In Caxton's *Chronicles,* an early history of England, King Richard II is described as an entrepreneur in battle. (Unfortunately, Richard II later succeeded in getting himself assassinated by his own knights. Talk about risk-taking!)

By the nineteenth century, the warrior connotation of *entrepreneur* had given way to a new, specialized meaning. The word was used to describe "the director or manager of a public musical institution" or "one who 'gets up' entertainments, especially musical performances." And so the definition of *impresario* stuck until sometime after World War II, when enterprising men and women began to take notice of the descriptive powers of *entrepreneur* once again. For a while, the word carried with it the sleazy connotation of fly-by-night profiteers sitting in badly-paneled offices with shag carpeting. But not for long. Just as shag carpeting and other tacky decorating features began disappearing in the 1970s and 1980s, so, too, did the downside associations of *entrepreneur.* As the smokestack economy began to give way to the Information Age, the New Entrepreneurs emerged as the leaders who would get us to the promised land of innovative thinking and healthy cash flow.

So the change from small business owner to entrepreneur represents far more than a mere change of nomenclature: it essentially bespeaks an important cultural shift. Small businesses hardly ever rode the cutting edge of societal megatrends. Entrepreneurial enterprises do. The owners of Mom and Pop grocery stores rarely became the subject of cover stories in *Newsweek*. Entrepreneurs do. In fact, our new obsession with entrepreneurial achievement reflects the general upscaling of America. For example, people used to eat carrot sticks from paper-bag lunches because root crops were cheap and good for them. Now they eat *crudités* at cocktail parties because they're a state-of-the-art hors d'oeuvre filled with precious fiber. The new entrepreneurs are to the small-business owners what *crudités* are to lowly carrot sticks. They're sexier, they're on the leading edge, and they're out to provide the fiber of the American mythology and economy.

To further understand the difference, consult the following:

The Essence of Entrechic

(or, How to avoid the small-business mind set)

Small businessperson owned	Entrepreneur owns
newsstand	pornographic software concern
luncheonette	multimillion-dollar stuffed-potato franchise operation
garment factory	licensing rights to Goretex sports brassiere line
worm farm	worm-protein ice cream enterprise
mink farm	national mink sperm bank and stud service network

4

THE ENTRECHIC QUESTIONNAIRE: DO YOU HAVE THE RIGHT STUFF?

Some people must work harder than others to adjust to the brave new world of mega-deals. Go with your gut feelings to answer the following questions about your entrepreneurial proclivities.

I. Background

1. I was born
   A. 1890–1929.
   B. 1930–1947.

C. 1948–1965.
D. 1966–1985.
2. Sex
   A. Male.
   B. Female.
   C. Often (ha, ha).
3. In grade school, I tried one or more of the following:
   A. Selling Girl Scout cookies.
   B. Selling lemonade.
   C. Selling glimpses of my underwear.
   D. Selling magazines.
   E. Selling my sibling.
   F. Selling life insurance.
4. During high school and college, I tried one or more of the following:
   A. Selling drugs.
   B. Buying penny stocks.
   C. Starting up a robotics firm.
   D. Manufacturing steroids.
   E. Marketing flavored condoms.
   F. Cloning the football team.
5. My father's profession was or is:
   A. Doctor, lawyer, accountant, dentist, President of the United States.
   B. Corporate manager or executive, government worker, minister or rabbi.
   C. Fireman, policeman, ventriloquist, acrobat, sanitation worker, barber, forest ranger.
   D. Gunslinger, confidence man, cat burglar, entrepreneur, Vietnamese refugee, professional hit man, lion trainer.

Access to Answers: *Question 1:* Entrepreneurial fever can strike at any age, so give yourself four points for A or B. But if you are a member of the Baby Boom or post-Baby Boom set (C and D), give yourself eight points. Under 21? Take ten points. *Question 2:* Entrepreneuring is macho work, so it's best to be male if possible. Give yourself three points if you're a guy and five points if you are of either sex and answered with C. (Entrepreneurs love to flout authority). *Questions 3 and 4:* Two points for each venture. *Question 5:* A dad in the D group will get you five points and make you the most likely candidate for entrepreneurship. For C, three points. For A or B, no points. If your *mother* worked at a C or D profession, add another five points.

Your entrescore so far: _____

II. Philosophy

Do you exhibit Type E entrepreneurial behavior traits? Complete the following sentences:

1. I am
    A. An okay person, but nothing special.
    B. Pretty damn good at what I do.
    C. One of the smartest people I know.
    D. Someone who can singlehandedly revolutionize an industry and the world.
2. I'd take a government job
    A. If it were offered to me.
    B. If I were forced.
    C. If it included regular meetings with the President of the United States and a chance to meet Frank Sinatra.
    D. When Hell freezes over.
3. People who work in 9-to-5 jobs are
    A. Just plain folks.
    B. The backbone of our society.
    C. Security-minded wimps.
    D. Losers sapping the economy of this country.
4. I would like to be my own boss because
    A. Entrepreneurship offers unlimited opportunity.
    B. I don't like to wear business suits.
    C. I want to make mega-millions.
    D. I'm a risk-taker who plans to become a household name.
5. My idea of a great hobby is
    A. Collecting stamps.
    B. Editing a video montage of Lite beer commercials.
    C. Scuba diving for photographic access to great white sharks.
    D. Base jumping off the World Trade Center.
6. I think working 90 hours a week
    A. Is nearly impossible.
    B. Would strain my personal relationships to the breaking point.
    C. Represents a good investment of sweat equity.
    D. Is a damn small price to pay for immortality.
7. If I found out my favorite lunchtime restaurant was about to go bankrupt, I would
    A. Offer my sympathy to the owner.
    B. Stop eating lunch.
    C. Find another luncheon spot not run by a loser.
    D. Form a corporation to buy out the owner and keep the place running.

8. If I lost a million dollars, I'd
   A. Shoot myself.
   B. Shoot a whole bunch of other people.
   C. Laugh and consider selling my vacation home.
   D. Sell my story to *Entrepreneur* magazine.

Access to Answers. For each question, give yourself zero points for answers A and B, five points for C, and seven points for D. Then give yourself a bonus of five points for risking the quiz thus far.

Your entrescore so far: _____

III. Vocabulary

Define the following terms:
1. Cellular mobile unit
   A. Portable blood bank.
   B. Prefab housing.
   C. Phone system for an automobile (preferably Mercedes or BMW).
2. Wozniak
   A. Polish brand of cherry cordial.
   B. One of the large furry creatures in *Star Wars*.
   C. One-half of the famous Apple Computer team.
3. IPO
   A. Interpersonal orgasm.
   B. International Police Organization.
   C. Initial public offering.
4. Mouse
   A. Dance invented by Soupy Sales.
   B. Foam for styling hair.
   C. Hand-held, photosensitive device for operating on-screen computer programs.
5. De-bug
   A. Jiminy Cricket's cousin.
   B. A new, nontoxic insecticide.
   C. To rid a product of major defects.
6. Skunk
   A. Punk hair style.
   B. Mafia term for informer.
   C. Corporate type who innovates products.
7. Intraprise
   A. Deep surprise.
   B. Innovative biofeedback program.
   C. Entrepreneurial project carried on within corporate walls.

8. Window
   A. Opening with clear glass.
   B. Much-advertised part of a software package.
   C. Specific unit of time allowing great opportunity.
9. Modem
   A. Sanitary protection for women.
   B. Carved American Indian symbol.
   C. Communications device for computer.
10. Joint venture
   A. Marijuana dealership.
   B. Hip replacement operation.
   C. Cooperative deal between companies or investors.

Access to Answers. For questions 1, 2, 3, 5, 6, 7, 9, and 10, give yourself five points for each C answer. If you had a gut feeling that questions 4 and 8 had more than one answer, you were correct. For 4, A and C are both correct; for 8, all three answers are correct.

Your entrescore so far: _____

IV. Lifestyle

1. Which of the following magazines do you read?
   □ *Success*
   □ *Venture*
   □ *In Business*
   □ *Money*
   □ *Forbes*
   □ *Fortune*
   □ *Inc.*
   □ *Sylvia Porter's Personal Finance*
   □ *Woman Entrepreneur (WE)*
   □ *Entrepreneur*
   □ *Soldier of Fortune*
2. How many times per year do you enter the lottery or sweepstakes?
   A. 0–2
   B. 3–15
   C. 16–100
   D. 101–500
3. How many times in the last year have you been to Atlantic City or Las Vegas?
   A. 0
   B. 1–3
   C. 4–25
   D. 26–100

4. How many different business cards do you own?
   A. 1
   B. 2–5
   C. 6–125
5. How many phone lines in your home?
   A. 1
   B. 2–5
   C. 6–25
6. Which of the following does your living space include?
   A. A basement.
   B. A garage.
   C. A spare bedroom or bathroom.
   D. An attic.
7. Which is your favorite 1960s rock group?
   A. The Supremes.
   B. The Rolling Stones.
   C. The Beatles.
   D. The Ventures.

Access to Answers. *Question 1:* Take three points for each of the first nine magazines. For *Entrepreneur* or *Soldier of Fortune,* subtract four points each. *Questions 2 and 3:* Two points for B, three for C, and six for D (good risk-taking training!). *Question 4:* The very entrechic own more than one enterprise. Take three points for B, five points for C. *Question 5:* The truly entrechic are communications-conscious. Take three points for B, five points for C. *Question 6:* Four points each for a basement or a garage, essential locations for small start-ups. Two points for the less adequate start-up space in C and D. *Question 7:* The little-known Ventures possess the perfect entrepreneurial name. Give yourself ten points if you had the good taste to pick them.

Your total entrescore: _____

The Mega-Results. How open are you to the concepts of entrepreneurial chic? Here are the numbers:
120–150: You're at the very top of the entrechic scale. Any venture capitalist would be happy to know you. Megabucks wait just around the corner.
85–119: You have the potential to join the Entrepreneurial Age, but you cling to security and still use phrases like "salary and benefits."
50–84: You are hopelessly out of touch with the innovative spirit of the 1980s. You must improve the thinking ability of your gut by quitting your time-based job and starting up a new enterprise. At the very least, buy a fast-food franchise.

49 and below: You're probably still sending away for the career school applications on the back of matchbook covers. Your idea of sweat equity is the money you spend on a Jane Fonda workout tape. **No score:** Congratulations! If you didn't have the patience to do the paperwork for these picayune questions, you possess the best mind set possible for entrepreneurial stardom. Tomorrow you will probably get a call from a business reporter.

ENTRY-LEVEL ENTREPRENEURS: TARGETING YOUR MARKET

Having determined your overall aptitude, now you must decide what field of enterprise will become the focus of your entrepreneurial savvy. Although thinking about what business to go into isn't as much fun as selecting the airport where you'll park your personal jet, the choice of market area is a necessary first step toward megabucks. The wealth of opportunity in the 1980s can confuse the would-be entrepreneur. As far as entrepreneurial chic goes, all enterprises are equal but some are more equal than others. We've rated market areas from lukewarm (one star) to steaming (two stars) to red-hot (three stars).

Restaurants: Becoming an Entréepreneur★★

"Everybody's gotta eat" used to be the words of encouragement offered to would-be restaurateurs. But the restaurant business long ago went beyond the simple function of providing sustenance. Food is now a very sexy commodity, and today's entréepreneurs can find themselves in the gossip sections of the daily newspaper and on the pages of business magazines.

To become an "in" place among the young professional *cognoscenti* who dine out more than 12 times a week, a new restaurant must have a striking concept. Gone are the days when steak and potatoes, Italian food, or burgers and beer served as a focus of a menu. It's even tough to get jaded diners excited about pasta, sushi, or filo dough creations. We recommend brainstorming cutting-edge culinary fads by thinking about what's caught on in the past. A budding restaurateur might consider combining implausible ingredients to attract publicity and curious consumers during the first few weeks of operation. For example, what about mashed potatoes and caviar? Sushi-filled calzones? Goat cheesecake?

CHECKLIST FOR THE ASPIRING ENTRÉEPRENEUR

Food. "Something old, something new" only works for weddings. Think new all the time, unless you can convince customers that something's so old it's new. (Witness how pot roast and pork chops have been dazzling New York palates of late.)

Decor. It helps to know either artists or owners of junkyards who can help you pull together a "concept" look.

Capital. You'll need a lot unless you're starting your restaurant on a pushcart or are convinced that you can grow all the ingredients for your recipes in your backyard.

Location. As one restaurateur puts it, "There are only three factors important in starting an eatery: location, location, and location."

Workforce. Employees are fairly transient and possess a nauseatingly high level of education. It's hard to fire a waitress with a Ph.D. who begins hurling Nietzschean epithets your way.

Support system. To succeed, it helps to have several restaurant critics and movie stars for friends.

Hazards of the trade. Obesity. Many restaurateurs later go on to start diet programs and health spas.

Patron saints of the entréepreneurs. Alfredo of fettuccine fame, Elaine, Vincent Sardi, Trader Vic, Wolfgang Puck, Alice Waters.

Five Reasons *Not* to Open Your Own Restaurant

1. You look good in a tuxedo.
2. Everybody likes your cheesecake.
3. You love eating out.

4. You already have a large salt and pepper shaker collection.
5. It seems fun.

High Tech: The State-of-the-Artrepreneur★★★

This red-hot market tantalizes with all an entrepreneur could ever hope for: millions when your company goes public, the cover of *Time,* and the possibility of becoming a household word. Unfortunately, it's also a field that usually requires some technical expertise. But don't let that stop you. It didn't stop Adam Osborne, who hired somebody to design his portable computer and then went on to enormous success and spectacular failure, all within three years.

In the silicon-laden high-tech circles, cashing in your "chips" takes on a whole new meaning. It's the only way to go for would-be entrepreneurs who want to make more than one hundred million in a year.

HIGH-TECH CHECKLIST

Product. Something invented by a brilliant nerd who will stay in the background and invent more things.
Location. California or other sunny locale. High-technoids are usually allergic to cold weather.

13

Places to start up venture. Garage, basement, incubator.
Jargon. Complex and exclusive.
Capital. From venture capitalists. You usually can't fund high-tech operations with a second mortgage on your house. Software enterprises are easy to start on a shoestring, but making hardware provides less chance for sweat equity because you can't build a computer with a Dixie cup and toothpicks.
Patron saints, or "star techs." Hewlett and Packard, Nolan Bushnell (Atari, Pizza Time Theater, etc.), William Gates (Microsoft Software), Steven Jobs (Apple), Stephen Wozniak (Apple), An Wang (Wang Laboratories), Adam Osborne, Lore Harp (Vector), Robert Noyce (Intel), Rod Canion (Compaq), David Kay (Kaypro), Mitch Kapor (Lotus Development Corp.).

Low Tech: High Concepts, Lowly Products*

Although low on the entrechic scale, this field offers a market where risk-takers can still make a killing if they want to. "Low tech" is an upscale term that embraces everything from clothing to cardboard boxes to fads such as Cabbage Patch dolls. Still confused? Here's the definition in a nutshell: Digging swimming pools is low tech. Inventing a robot to take care of swimming pools is high tech.

Advocates of the low-tech route to entrepreneurial success point out that it is wide open to new ideas, many of which do not immediately become obsolete six months later because of technological changes. (However, some products become obsolete after three months since everyone in America received one or more for Christmas.)

LOW-TECH CHECKLIST

Examples of types of businesses. Direct-mail catalog, dog-food stores, housepainting, furniture sales, hardware (as in tools, *not* computers!), games, singing telegram companies, stupid but expensive novelty items.
Patron saints. Scott Abbot, Chris Haney, John Haney, and Ed Werner (Trivial Pursuit); Richard Knerr and Arthur Melin (Hula

Hoop and Frisbee); Xavier Roberts (Cabbage Patch doll); Gary Dahl (Pet Rock); Marvin Wernick (Mood Ring).

Food Fads: Snack and Beverage Magnates★★★

Baby-Boomers hunger for rehabilitated versions of the junk food of their youths. For the last five years, entrepreneurs have been making their fortunes on chocolate chip cookies, oreo ice cream, and various and sundry other "comfortable" snack foods. The cookie trend seems to have played itself out (the Chipwich, a combination of cookies and ice cream, represents a last gasp at modifying those two foods). The hottest new fad food field is now the beverage industry, where natural sodas and wine punches are gaining market shares.

Ease of start-up remains the biggest advantage of this field. At first, you can even use your own kitchen. But make sure the health inspector doesn't see your dog Spot get up and lick the baking dish. And watch out for flies in the wine punch.

Once you get started, the entrechic opportunities are almost unlimited. Food fad entrepreneurs are in great demand for media interviews, since their products are a lot easier to explain than software programs. And everybody likes the homey aspects of snack entrepreneurship (even if the homey quality is totally fake).

Patron saints: Famous Amos (cookies), Mrs. (Debbi) Fields (cookies), David Liederman (David's Cookies), Mo J. Siegel (Celestial Seasonings tea), Sharon Corr (Corr's Sodas), Michael M. Crete and R. Stuart Bewley (California Cooler).

Biotech: The Blue Genes Entrepreneur★★★

Thanks to modern science, entrepreneurs can now have a say in the genetic makeup of the human race. Do you have an idea that would work well in a Petri dish? Or how about a new native birth control product discovered on your latest vacation trip to the New Zealand outback? The biotechpreneur has not only the satisfaction of fame and fortune, but also the knowledge that he can fool with the human body just as well as big corporations can.

A genetics company going public is almost as sexy as a high-tech concern, so if you were good in high school biology, consider this field of enterprise.

BIOTECH CHECKLIST

Regulatory problems. The Federal Drug Administration is always hassling biotechnoids, making them prove their results.

Legal problems. People love to sue the makers of pharmaceutical products.

Location. Genetic imaginations run most free in California. (How do you think they got all those blue-eyed blondes out there? Those genetics firms have been working undercover for years.)

Capital. Mostly venture capital. But you can raise money by running a Nobel Laureate sperm bank in your basement.

Patron saints. Robert Swanson (Genentech), Bruce Vorhauer (inventor of Today contraceptive sponge, VLI Corporation).

Real Estate: The Entrepreneurial Landed Gentry★

Wheeling and dealing in real estate would be a hot field if it weren't so anonymous. Many entrepreneurs make real estate a second career after they've sold the first enterprise. Others take small family holdings and expand them beyond Grandpa's wildest dreams. This is a good field for "trust fund entrepreneurs," who have a little of their own capital to start with. But with the aid of handy books like Robert Allen's *Nothing Down,* even uncapitalized entrepreneurs can dabble in real estate deals.

Strong-willed types particularly enjoy designing "concept" developments or creating a "renaissance" area in a city.

REAL ESTATE CHECKLIST

Tip. When real estate entrepreneurs say "syndicate," they're not referring to the Mafia.

Patron saints. William J. Levitt, Sam Lefrak, Leona Helmsley (gets to dress up as a queen in her hotel ads), Donald Trump (even struck oil on some of his land in New York City).

The Infopreneurial Consulting Biz★★

The rise of the computer data base has contributed to the growth in the number of entrepreneurs who sell information to companies and individuals. This information can take the form of special consulting reports, newsletters, or trend lists. Infopreneurs get their data from newspapers, government pamphlets, interviews with average citizens, and the backs of cereal boxes. Most charge at least $1,000 for an idea of any significance.

Entrepreneurs who specialize in business consulting introduce companies to startling concepts, such as "You must reward employees if you want them to continue working for you."

INFOTECH CHECKLIST

Capital and start-up. For information consulting, all you need are four newspaper subscriptions, a pair of scissors, and a phone booth nearby. Would-be business consultants should call their mothers to learn some common sense clichés they can resell immediately.

Advantages. High visibility. If lucky, you'll write one best seller and never have to consult again. You can spend your days on the lecture circuit.

Patron saints. Alvin Toffler (*Future Shock*), John Naisbitt (*Megatrends*), Carole Jackson (*Color Me Beautiful*), Thomas J. Peters and Robert H. Waterman, Jr. (*In Search of Excellence*), Kenneth Blanchard and Spencer Johnson (*One Minute Manager*), Rosabeth Moss Kanter (*The Change Masters*), Robert Schwartz (School for Entrepreneurs, Tarrytown, NY), Gifford Pinchot III (*Intrapreneuring*).

17

More Megatrendy Ideas

If none of the others inspire brainstorms, here are some additional megatrendy products and fields, also rated on the entrechic scale:

Airlines (especially no-frills)★★★
Magazine publishing★★
Oil and natural gas companies★★
Cosmetics★
Chemicals★
Express mail★★
Cable television★★
Movie production★★
Retail franchises★

RISK, THE ENTREPRENEUR'S HOLY GRAIL

In all entrepreneurial fields offering the best access to fame and fortune, one element dominates: risk. The very entrechic are hooked on taking chances the way other people are hooked on cocaine. An obsession with a high risk level pervades work lives, leisure time, and conversations. "Risk-taker" is the highest accolade in entrepreneurial circles. Caught up in gamesmanship, entrepreneurs love thinking that every business decision represents a choice between the life and death of their enterprises. You'll frequently hear this new breed of junkies brag about their courtship of fickle Fate. Good entrepreneurs are never happier than when faced with the possibility of losing millions of dollars, a good reputation, or both. And the risk-taking spirit doesn't get left at the office. When entrechic types unwind, they choose dangerous hobbies such as mountain climbing or hang gliding to hone their skills of chance.

If you're not naturally prone to taking chances, don't worry. You *can* develop the nerve it takes to laugh in the face of total economic ruin. Just try some of these simple exercises, and soon you'll find yourself walking in front of cars or starting a company.

SIX EASY STEPS TO CONFIDENT RISK-TAKING

1. Throw away all dry cleaner receipts right after dropping off the clothing.
2. Drive on superhighways in a Honda Civic and make obscene gestures at truck drivers.
3. Call the IRS and request an audit.
4. Make all your sandwiches with unsealed jars of room-temperature mayonnaise.
5. Buy a pet cobra.
6. Wing-walk during your next business flight.

ENTREVIEW

One in a series of conversations
with leading-edge entrepreneurs

Stuart Careers of Orange
Computers, Inc.

Once a student of a Mahareeshi, college dropout Stuart Careers built a personal computer in his garage that revolutionized the industry. Careers is now president of Orange Computers, which went public several years ago and made him a multimillionaire. He remains closely involved in every aspect of the company. In fact, when our Entrechic reporter found him, he was out in the shop tinkering with a souped-up version of the company's newest product, the Tangelo personal computer. Other parts of the interview took place over lunch, in his Porsche, and during a photo session for a major newsmagazine.

Entrechic: *I guess we'd like to begin by asking you what everybody's dying to know.*

Careers: No, I don't have a girlfriend. Geez, everyone always asks me that. No, I don't. I'm not seeing anyone. And I don't care. You want to know why? Because I'm making the world better every single day. Yes, I'm making it better by building people the most wonderful computers ever made. So who cares if I don't have a girlfriend? I'm only twenty-eight, for Chrissakes. I mean, I have plenty of time. So I'm a late bloomer. I mean, you can't make the world a better place and have girlfriends and everything.

EC: *Um, that's very interesting, but actually, we were going to ask why you named your company Orange Computers.*

Careers: Oh. Let's see. I guess it was because people like oranges and they have vitamin C and good stuff like that. There's lots of them out here in California. Also, as I remember, my friend who was the marketing guy pushed for it. Before Hertz snapped up O. J. Simpson, we were going to have him pitch a machine called The Juice.

EC: *Yes, I guess having a concept name for your company really aids in future brainstorming sessions for new product names.*

Careers: It sure does. Even the products that never make it to market get more enthusiasm in-house when we give them a catchy name in their early stages. For example, there was our round-shaped keyboard and mouse set that worked like a Ouija board. A real high-concept idea, but well before its time. Around here, we called it The Orange Bowl.

EC: *You mention new products. How much does the culture of the community you're located in—Database Dell—contribute to the atmosphere of innovation at Orange Computers?*

21

Careers: It makes all the difference in the world. This is the hub of the American computer and software industry. Plus everybody's under thirty-five. It would be weird to be in a regular place where people have prostate problems and hardening of the arteries. I imagine it would really cut down on the productivity.

EC: How do you see the future of the computer industry now that some of the large companies have stepped into the market and, indeed, dominated it?
Careers: They're just bullies. I know we can lick 'em. Americans love the little guy. That's why I'm not worried. Already, sales of our Tangelo computer are helping us recapture market share. By the way, did you see our new television commercial with guys in three-piece suits trying to cut down an orange tree? That's really how we all feel about those corporate types. Those big guys don't really care about people or making the world a better place. We do. (*At this point, Careers paused to look at his Mickey Mouse watch.*) Hey, do you mind if we end this? I've enjoyed talking to you, but at three o'clock I always get together with a few of the guys in the prototype lab to watch *He Man* cartoons.

2

THE ENTREPRENEUR'S I.D.: IDEAS AND DEALS

For the true entrepreneur, the most exciting stage in the process of building an enterprise is the time before and immediately after start-up, when everything seems possible. The newness of the venture and the courtship of potential employees, customers, and financial backers mimic the first few months of a love affair. The potential entrepreneur enjoys boundless energy, thinks about the beloved business every minute of the day, and can't eat or sleep.

Try to make the most of this initial phase. Some venturers never get over the sexy high they feel during this period. When the honeymoon is over and the long marriage to the company has simmered down to a steady drone of dull detail, the restless entrepreneur sells or freaks out and leaves to start up another company. This approach is fine if you're not hooked on having a high public profile. However, for ultimate entrechic gains, stay until the company is in proper shape to go public. Then sell it for a tidy sum to a huge conglomerate that will keep you on as a jet-setting consultant.

But don't start counting your millions yet. First, you must go through the process of getting and implementing an idea. Ideas, or "concepts," are the currency of entrepreneurship. You'll need to know how to brainstorm your way to a successful venture. Yet the concept phase means nothing if you can't cut the proper deal afterward. Having achieved the proper combination of brainstorming and deal-cutting, you will have earned your I.D. as an entrepreneur.

BRAINSTORMING THE CONCEPT

Usually, a chic entrepreneur will have decided on a market area before tackling the concept for a new enterprise (see Chapter 1). For example, if the role of restaurateur appeals, you need only narrow it down to the gimmick your restaurant will use to lure trendy eaters. If you have a yen for the high-tech field, you'll at least know that you should be brainstorming about silicon and circuitry, not nuts and bolts.

Occasionally, you won't have the slightest idea what area of commerce you prefer to enhance with your verve and style. Don't despair. Some of the best entrepreneurial concepts are stumbled over by confused and desperate people who finally "hit the big one." There's no reason you can't, too. But we suggest going about it more systematically than the average Joe or Jane if you are really aiming to make the cover of *Forbes* or *Newsweek* someday.

Before you begin brainstorming, remember the cardinal rules of concept generation:

1. You should be able to explain your concept to venture capitalists or anyone with a third-grade education within five minutes. This makes it a "high concept."
2. If someone doesn't understand your concept, call your mother. She won't either, but she'll always pretend.
3. You can never be too paranoid. If a person has a savings account with more than one hundred dollars in it, don't tell him about your idea—he's likely to abscond with it.

The art of concept brainstorming can be practiced alone or in collaboration with others you trust or keep handcuffed in your closet. The hours between three and six in the morning are prime time for the really great generation of ideas. Necessary props for early-morning sessions are half-empty bottles of Scotch or brandy. You'll notice as you get more adept at storming your brain that the kicking around of ideas falls into several broad strategic categories.

Types of Brainstorming Strategies

Reactive. Some major event spurs ideas about possible products or services for which the public will soon begin clamoring. Most low-tech impulse products get birthed in this way. For example, after a New York state law was passed requiring the wearing of seat belts, some savvy entrepreneurs began marketing a T-shirt that makes people look like they're wearing a restraint even if they aren't.

Technological. Inventive types stay up on the state-of-the-art gadgets and find a niche where their skills and a market can match. This is a variation of the clichéd "build a better mousetrap" strategy. Soon it will be called "build a better mouse."

Imitative. Practitioners of this sort of brainstorming are true masochists who greet word of every new invention or windfall profit with the anguished cry, "Why not me, why not me?" They often are fond of telling anyone who will listen that they had an idea first but just never got the backing. ("You know that phone-answering machine stuff? I thought of that years ago. Yeah, I have one drawn in my notebook.") This is the most self-defeating type of brainstorming, but stealing formulas or ideas and changing them only slightly represents the highest art form in certain industries, such as television production, moviemaking, and electronics.

Fitting the Concept into the Time Framework

A concept can be the best in the world, but it won't fly if the time isn't right. Judging whether your idea will be in sync with the moment is one of the hardest parts of becoming a savvy entrepreneur. "He was before his time" is a wonderful thing to say about statesmen and dead poets, but it isn't any good as a compliment to entrepreneurs. Similarly, no entrepreneur wants to hear that his idea is one that's already come and gone.

How do you know if a concept "speaks to" the times? How do you tell if your product or service will make it on Zeitgeist appeal? You don't. But you can try your damnedest to be well-acquainted with demographic and societal trends in order to ensure your concept its best possible environment for fruition. In this, as in all your endeavors, you must *Think Mega!* Truly successful entrepreneurs are always taking the pulse of America and figuring out what trend will sweep the country in the next few years.

We've prepared this chart explaining how to brainstorm according to societal trends and realities. None of the products suggested has caught on yet, but it's only a matter of time.

Turning Trends into Megabucks

Societal Trend or Truth	Entrepreneurial Concept
More women are keeping their birth names after marriage.	Dual-monogramming machine.
Young children get their clothes filthy.	Nudist day care center.
People are increasingly obsessed with self-improvement.	Best seller: *Thirty Days to a Beefier Brain.*
Reading skills are declining nationwide.	Video obituary cable channel.

Spot the Lemon

An entrepreneur on the lookout for the Concept of the Century comes in contact with hundreds of ideas that seem at first glance plausible and lucrative. But just as we usually don't marry the first person we go out with, an aspiring risk-taker should guard against impulsive venturing.

Some of the telltale signs that identify a concept or product as a possible lemon are:

1. The inventor's untimely expulsion from another country.
2. The product's appearance in late night TV ads.

Other than these warning signals, you're on your own when trying to weed out impossible schemes from possible moneymaking ventures. A good clue that you've picked a lemon is that the venture capitalists you meet with start laughing hysterically or choking on their lunchtime entrées.

A CAPITAL IDEA: VENTURING FORTH FOR FUNDS

Whatever the idea, sooner or later you're going to have to get some seed money to implement it. This can be as simple as borrowing a couple of thousand from Mom and Dad or as complicated as seeking millions from the new breed of venture capitalists. Proper capitalization isn't all that different than when you were in grade school: You must learn to take your concept and put it *in big letters*. You must convince your wife, husband, banker, or other backer that your enterprise will pan out in the end.

This task isn't as easy as it sounds, even if you are very charming. The woods are filled with idea-laden entrepreneurs on the trail of start-up funds. Here is some basic advice for seeking each of the levels of start-up capital available on the business scene.

The Levels of Capitalization

Level One: A quick loan from friends or family. Guilt is a good method here. Start by saying things like, "You'll never forgive yourself if you ruin my one big chance to make it." If that doesn't work, get yourself fired from your job and then open up a lemonade stand in front of your house or apartment building. Most loved ones will reach for their wallets when they see a grown man or woman reduced to selling Dixie cups full of a ten-cent soft drink. Unfortunately, this sort of minor capital is suitable *only* for pushcarts, mail-order businesses, aerobic dance studios, and some consulting businesses.

Level Two: A second mortgage on the house. Your spouse or significant other needs convincing in this situation. Bring up the subject by talking about how some couples have two houses, and you only have one. Tell her or him to think of the second mortgage as a maintenance-free vacation home. Then say wistfully, "If only I could own my own ice cream store/communications company/trash service, I'd never be unhappy again."

Level Three: A substantial loan from your bank. Histrionic skills come into play here as you paint a picture of the world as a better place once your company springs into being. You must make your loan officer feel she's part of a larger mission in life. Of course, you'll have to get up some kind of business plan to make her feel comfortable, too. On your first meeting, mention how much you admire the bank's reputation for risk-taking, even if the last major loan they made was for the purchase of an Edsel.

Level Four: The Big League, or Venture Capital. Sometimes regular bank loans just aren't enough, especially if you've found the cure for cancer, invented a new computer software program, or brainstormed the latest Madonna spinoff product. That's when it's time to call in the pros, the venture capitalists. In return for a share of equity or a pound of your flesh, these high-tech Shylocks will facilitate your start-up or help your company grow. Naturally, they'll want to know all about your plans before they agree to invest. Sometimes they also want your first-born child. An entrepreneurial caveat: Beware if a venture capitalist demands to be a beneficiary of your life insurance policy and then takes an unhealthy interest in your skydiving hobby.

Courting the Venture Gods

Getting money out of a venture capitalist might seem to be a sophisticated, modern transaction. Actually, it's a bit akin to ancient fertility rituals in which men prayed to the gods to grant them favorable growing conditions. You, the entrepreneur, don special, ceremonial clothing to visit the Venture Gods. There are a great number of them, and you must make oblations to as many as will let you in the door. You make paper offerings with strange symbols written on them. You dance around a lot and boast mightily about your prowess as a warrior in the marketplace. Sometimes, if you're lucky, the Gods invite you to drink firewater.

Then you must go away for a long time. The Gods consider what to do. Some entrepreneurs get rewarded with seed money for cash crops. Others lapse into poverty and despair, unable to cut a deal.

Usually, it's those paper offerings with the strange symbols that ultimately capture the attention of the Venture Gods. Entrepreneurs call them business plans. They use them to impress the Gods with big words and phrases about their enterprises. The Gods particularly like plans that say things like "a concept that will change the course of civilization," "broad market appeal," and "revolutionary."

Games
Venture Capitalists and
Entrepreneurs Play

If entrepreneurs make lots of money, the first thing they like to do (even *before* they buy a jet) is to become Venture Gods, too. That way, they get to see others squirm the way they squirmed at the altar of venture capital.

The Entrepreneur's new clothes. An entrepreneur pretends to have a fully clothed concept when his company is still but a gleam in his eye. Tricks of the trade include renting a factory and staffing it with friends just before the venture capitalist comes to call. When dining with venture capitalists, the wily entrepreneur might also try having himself paged with a message from another venture capital firm.

Entrepreneur "Gong Show." Some venture capitalists cooperate with business groups to do public cattlecalls of companies and inventors in need of capital. The nervous entrepreneur gets to make a presentation and then see his or her concept ripped to shreds by a panel of experts. These entrepreneurial amateur hours take place in cities around the country.

The Dating Game. Services, some of them nonprofit, some of them not, match up entrepreneurs who have the concepts with venture capitalists who have the megabucks. These high-tech matchmakers could be called the Pimps of Progress.

WHO ARE THESE VENTURE CAPITALISTS, ANYWAY?

The people who hold the real power on the entrepreneurial scene today are venture capitalists (VCs). Before the 1970s, loaning seed money for new companies or capital for ongoing concerns was a wimp profession peopled by brats from rich families who needed a hobby. Offering capital in exchange for equity in small companies was a way to get their kicks and supplement their trust funds.

But the days of venture capital as a gentleman's profession are long gone. Today's VC is one of a brash breed of movers and shakers who often boasts an MBA *and* the expertise to actually understand the high-tech fields he's investing in. He jets around the country looking for lucrative start-ups. The word "salary" never passes his lips. He lives for the ROI (return on investment). He eats unprepared entrepreneurs for breakfast. Some sensitive souls might say that he's a vulture capitalist, but he's laughing all the way to the bank. He's the Clint Eastwood of entrechicdom, saying to each entrepreneur in search of funds, "Go ahead, make my day."

PROFILE OF A VENTURE CAPITALIST

A VC is usually:
Male
Macho as hell
Opinionated
Slim
Unsentimental
Rich
Everyone who graduates from Harvard Business School would like to be a VC someday. A guy with an overabundance of entrechic can grow up to become both a successful entrepreneur and a VCR— a venture capitalist retread—who assists others with start-up funds.

BUSINESS ORGANIZATION: PLANNING FOR THE FUTURE

When first conceptualizing your enterprise, you'll be faced with the very important question of form. Should your venture be a proprietorship, a partnership, a private corporation, or a public offering? Obviously, there are benefits and pitfalls to each venture genre.

Choosing a Corporate Infrastructure

A sole proprietorship works well for small retail businesses, restaurants, and some service-oriented enterprises. The tax breaks are not the best, but as an individual owner, you have the freedom to do just about anything you want. If by some chance the enterprise should fail, you can also fade pretty quietly into the woodwork. But it's also hard to think mega when you're only a proprietor and not a CEO. To be absolutely frank, a proprietorship rates rather low on the entrepreneurial status scale. Better to start out as a proprietor with an eye toward franchising or building a holding corporation for a chain of businesses.

The partnership is a tricky organizational form that confers about the same amount of status as a proprietorship along with the bonus of possible ruined friendships. Very few people survive a partnership without some rough times, especially if they were close friends with their business partners B.S.U. (before start-up). If you want to jump head first into the world of entrechic, we recommend the next step up, the private corporation.

Ah, the magic of that little abbreviation, "Inc."! Most savvy entrepreneurs prefer incorporation because it provides the best chance to do everything the big boys do. You can pick titles, choose a board from among colleagues and old college sweethearts, and select from an array of tax evasion strategies. Your business cards look better when you're a corporation. And, if you're lucky enough to go public at the very beginning or soon after your blessed enterprise gets going, you can enjoy knowing that all those stockholders out there also believe in your dream. Incorporation is the only way to go for the serious pursuer of entrepreneurial chic.

Naming Your Enterprise

Large corporations pay thousands of dollars to consultants who come up with catchy names for automobiles, computers, and laundry detergents. Even though you will be a millionaire some day, chances are you don't have the resources to hire a pro to name your company. So think carefully, because a name means everything to the success of your enterprise.

First, let's consider your prior experience in naming things and see if we can draw any conclusions. You've probably named pets. What strategies did you use? Are you an innovative pet-namer, or did you settle for Fido, Spot, Kitty, or Princess? Are you one of those pretentious snobs who insists on calling cats and dogs by the names of characters in medieval romances and nineteenth-century novels? Or do you enjoy calling animals by nerdy human appellations, such as Ralph, Fred, or Frank? Any of these approaches indicates that you will have problems with naming a high-tech company, restaurant, or consulting concern. Calling a software concern "Stanley" will alienate a significant percentage of consumers. You might get away with calling a restaurant "Chaucer's," but "The Wife of Bath Biotech Co." won't work. And following the usual run-of-the-mill names for a company isn't a good strategy, either. You're liable to get sued if you call a new enterprise IBM or General Electric.

If you've reached the parental stage of life, you've probably had even more experience in the naming department. Unfortunately, your tyke-dubbing skills will not help in naming a business operation. Otherwise, we'd have dozens of mail-order catalogs called Joshua, or hundreds of Caitlin Computer companies. Remember, Coleco tried naming a computer Adam, with such disastrous results that they've abandoned the whole high-tech field in favor of Cabbage Patch dolls. So what's a name-seeking entrepreneur to do? Actually, there are several simple factors to take into consideration. Just make sure that the name you choose for your venture contains one or more of the special features listed below.

HIGH-TECH PREFIXES AND SUFFIXES

Good ones to consider are cellu-, intel-, mega-, micro-, spectra-, tek-, tele-, tech-, medi-, bio-, -byte, -tronics, -technic, -matrix, and -flex. These can be used with each other or with other nouns to create a catchy name for your beloved venture. A good trick is to capitalize each component of a compound name, as in BioVenture, Micro-Squoosh, or TeleCheesesteak.

EXOTIC OR COUNTERCULTURE WORDS

Lotus Development Corp., a software company, is a prime example of the trend toward choosing names with a definite ring of 1960s nostalgia to them. Play around with other words and phrases from that era. How about Tie-dye Technology, CelluKarma, Mantra Microchips, Brown Rice Concepts, AshramWare, Horoscope Robotics, Hare Krishna Designs, Kent State-of-the-Art, Attica Food Shoppe, Kill the Pigs Party Consultants?

REGIONAL APPELLATIONS

Regionalism is in, and entrepreneurs have done their part to contribute to its glamor. You're in luck if you come from any of the trendy states such as Texas, Minnesota, or California. Just pick a town name or some descriptive attribute for your company name. Even if you live in a dumpy place, you can still show regional pride with a cute local name. One New Jersey company calls itself Jersey Cow Software. Don't be shy. Experiment with the same clichés used on state license plates. Sooner Software? Hoosier Tech? Live Free or Die Inc.?

YOUR OWN NAME

To reinforce a spiritual marriage to the enterprise, you might want to give your beloved start-up your very own name. Adam Osborne did it with his computer company. So did An Wang. In the egotistical company of other entrepreneurs, you hardly need worry about modesty. A partial option, similar to having your wife or husband hyphenate a surname, is the combination of some part of your name with the names of your business partners or with one of the high-tech prefixes or suffixes. Try Houlihantech, Smithatron, SpectraJones, or BioJoeFredEddy.

What to Call Yourself

Equally important as a name for your enterprise is the title you get to make up for yourself. Even before rounding up capital, one of your first priorities should be business cards proudly displaying your rank as Chief Person.

Possible titles for the Entrepreneur: President, Chief Executive Officer, Director, Founding Director, Executive Director, Chairman of the Board, Owner, Head Facilitator (for nonhierarchical types). **Titles to avoid:** His Royal Highness, The Exalted One, Queen, Omnipotent Leader, Sultan, Ayatollah.

INEFFICIENT AND UNCHIC WAYS TO RAISE SEED CAPITAL

Selling sperm or a vital organ.
Rolling extra pennies.
Dealing cocaine.
Playing the violin outside theaters.
Kidnapping a successful entrepreneur's child.
Getting an advance for an autobiography.
Playing the lottery.
Advertising in the back of Arabic magazines.
Going on game shows.
Waiting for a rich relative to "kick."

GETTING STARTED ON YOUR START-UP

Once you have the money, the name, and your own title, it's time to get the show on the road. Entrepreneurs don't begin anything, they *start up*. Use this phrase as a noun, adjective, and verb constantly during the first three years of your operation. For some, the start-up period of a new enterprise is a painful time best forgotten. For others, it's the only part they really enjoy, because they get to do impossible things like work 23 hours a day and answer the phone in regional accents to simulate a large office staff.

Types of Start-ups

Whatever your attitude toward start-up, the beginning phase of your company or enterprise might fall into one of these categories.

The kick-start-up. This type usually occurs when a would-be entrepreneur is kicked out of a comfortable job and vows revenge. A mad scramble for product or service ideas ensues, along with frantic searches for capital. For the first few months, it seems impossible that the whole deal will come together. About the time she or he is looking longingly at the late-night television ads for computer training possibilities, everything falls into place, and the entrepreneur kick-starts the enterprise.

The head-start-up. The entrepreneur already has a fully operational company that is about to go public. There's only one problem: it's all in his or her head. These types fantasize about sales orders while the rest of us think about Caribbean beaches. Occasionally, a head-start-up can actually be translated to reality, but it's usually a disappointment for the entrepreneur, since real life is never as much fun as imaginary deal-cutting.

The false-start-up. Fairly self-explanatory. These types occur when the entrepreneurs get seed money that fails to germinate. Or when what the entrepreneur thought was a megatrend turns out to be a microblip on the cardiogram of popular culture.

The fresh-start-up. Often practiced by those who have been through several false-start-ups, this is a type for those who just keep plugging along. Their business brain is a *tabula rasa,* their optimism endless. "Tomorrow's another day" is the unofficial anthem of the fresh-start-up crowd, who believe that anyone in America can make a million if they get a good night's sleep and a fresh start in the morning.

The stop-and-start-up. The daily operation of the company depends on whether or not any checks arrive in the mail on a given day. Phone-answering machines are a boon to this halting type of start-up, since stop-and-start entrepreneurs can pretend they've just stepped out to lunch when in reality they've halted production for three weeks.

Putting All Your Eggs in One Basket: The Incubator

Companies in the throes of start-up can now huddle in specially designed working spaces called incubators. Often sponsored by local Chambers of Commerce or universities, incubators offer low rent, office furniture and equipment, and sometimes office staff to beginning enterprises. Should you consider incubating your enterprise before hatching it into a multimillion-dollar nest egg? Think carefully before committing yourself, and consult the following checklists of advantages and disadvantages.

THE UPSIDE OF INCUBATORS

★ Low overhead.
★ Camaraderie with other entrepreneurial types. (It's nice to see other people at the Coke machine at one in the morning. Single entrepreneurs, take note: a good way to find dates with plenty of entrechic.)
★ Prestigious address. (University towns show foreign movies. Everyone knows that.)

★ Good press opportunities. (If one of your colleagues' companies hits it big, the reporters will be sniffing around and just might knock on your door.)

THE DOWNSIDE OF INCUBATORS

★ Tacky-looking office. (Not conducive to impressing potential clients.)
★ Nomenclature. Doctors put premature babies in incubators. Some entrepreneurs balk at the comparison.
★ Psychological competition with other entrepreneurial types. ("My company's bigger than your company, so there!")
★ Dormitory atmosphere increases the feeling that you are an adolescent company not big enough to be on your own yet.

The jury's out on whether incubators are truly hotbeds of entrechic. They're not quite downscale enough to match the reverse chic of a basement or a garage, and they're not upscale enough to inspire mega-thoughts. But go with your gut. If you need a good start-up atmosphere and you're living in an apartment house with no access to a basement, check out incubative quarters.

ENTREQUOTE

"I want to go back to the garage where you don't have to fill out a dozen forms to get something done."

Stephen Wozniak, talking about why he left Apple Computer.

LOOKING AHEAD TO THE END-UP PHASE

In between start-ups and end-ups, there's not a whole lot of exciting stuff that goes on in an entrepreneur's daily life. You're not likely to get much media attention, for example, until your enterprise is pretty close to the end-up phase. And most of the downside events of entrepreneurship take place during the in-between period (see Chapter 3). So, even while you are still in the brainstorming or start-up phase, start planning the type of spectacular end-up you expect for your venture. And, if you decide that you'd rather end up at your company forever rather than face a formal end-up, you should know about your option to go public.

How to Stop Minding Your Own Business

1. EXERCISING YOUR FRANCHISE

You're well past the successful start-up phase, making money hand over fist with a Nickel Buffalo Burger stand. Or your Colorful Canine Consulting firm for fashion-conscious pets has more clients than it can handle. Chances are you're ready to franchise. You can offer franchises for sale or bring in a franchising service to help package your concept for go-getters across the country. Better yet, unload the concept and several units for a couple of million bucks to a large corporation and let executives worry about expanding a franchise operation.

2. SELLING OUT

Cashing in sweat equity and taking early retirement is an excellent way to preserve an entrechic image. Those attracted to this strategy think of themselves as athletes retiring at the prime of their careers. Of course, there's also no shame in taking those capital gains and starting all over again, which is what many of the entrepreneurially inclined do. Just make sure you keep playing well and making more megamillions each time you sell out. There's a certain amount of grace involved in getting out while the getting's good. Remember Muhammed Ali and Bobby Riggs.

3. GOING UNDER

Not recommended, but it's another method for getting away from it all. The major drawback is the lack of personal megamillions traditionally associated with bankruptcy. However, you might want to take out an ad in *The New York Times* pleading for donations for legal expenses. This sort of action preserves your entrechic image even under duress.

How to Keep Minding Your Own Business

Folks who can't entirely make the break from the 9-to-5 existence also have the option of bringing their enterprise into the mainstream of the business world.

1. GOING PUBLIC

Going public represents another route to extreme personal wealth that allows you to accumulate a hefty chunk of company stock while staying on as president, CEO, or Supreme Ruler. Although selling off chunks of a company to an eager public undeniably qualifies as the pinnacle of the entrechic experience for many entrepreneurs, going public has major downside aspects, too. For one, the CEO usually can't sell short any large quantities of shares without getting in trouble with the SEC, that pesky agency that worries about things like insider information. Moreover, any divestiture of stock will make your loyalties suspect. So you become a paper mega-millionaire, which isn't nearly as much fun as being a real one.

Think carefully before taking your enterprise public. It's annoying enough that heads of privately held companies must suffer the petty interference of venture capitalists who want to sit on the board and hold the purse strings. After going public, you'll have to contend with thousands of gadflies who will have the gall to actually think they own some of your venture just because they have a few stock certificates in the safe deposit box.

2. STAYING EXACTLY THE SAME

This complacent nongrowth strategy automatically keeps you from ever joining the ranks of the entrechic. No owner of one takeout Cornish hen shop ever made the cover of *Forbes*. A computer company that produces 25 quality machines a year will never get its owner an invitation to the White House, either.

ENTREPRATTLE: AN ANNOTATED GLOSSARY OF ENTRECHIC TERMS

Like every other distinct lifestyle, the entrepreneurial existence comes with a dialect all its own. Sprinkle your speech with some of these terms to achieve an entrepreneurially chic image.

access, *n.* an entranceway or opportunity, as in "I need access to the market!" Also verb, as in "Can you access that information?"

basement, *n.* one of the places where entrepreneurial empires begin. See also *garage*.

brainstorm, *v.* to sit around either alone or in the company of others and throw out preposterous ideas for discussion.

chip, *n.* whether chocolate or silicon, the basic component of many an entrepreneurial product.

concept, *n.* upscale term for *idea*. A *high concept* takes only a sentence to explain; a *low concept* needs at least a sixth-grade education to understand.

culture, *n.* the attitude and atmosphere of a company you admire or run. Most entre-prises strive for the nonhierarchical culture.

deal, *n.* the basic business transaction. Usually used with verb *to cut*.

deal-killer, *n.* lawyer.

enterprise, *n.* a business or other lucrative venture. A somewhat archaic word that infiltrated business vocabulary via *Star Trek* reruns.

entrepreneuse, *n.* female entrepreneur.

entropy, *n.* terrible mental disease suffered by entrepreneurs; a version of burnout in which sufferer's mind is filled with chaos.

excellence, *n.* what everyone is in search of.

garage, *n.* good location for start-up. Especially used in California, where earthquakes prevent the building of basements.

going public, *n.* "coming out of the closet" to sell company shares to the public for enormous economic gain. The stuff of which entrepreneurial dreams are made. See also *IPO*.

gut, *n.* major thinking organ of many entrepreneurs. As in "I can feel it in my gut." Also *adjective: gut* feeling, *gut* hunch.

hacker, *n.* what a high-tech entrepreneur calls himself before becoming a millionaire.

heart, *n.* indefinable quality of gumption inherent in entrepreneurial personalities. Seldom used with "You gotta have . . ."

Hewlett and Packard, *n.* the Jobs and Wozniak of the 1940s.

high-tech, *adj.* field or product requiring silicon chips and three or more engineers to explain it.

Horatio Alger, *n.* the Steven Jobs of the nineteenth century.

incubator, *n.* facility with support staff and office equipment at cheaper rates for start-up businesses. Particularly favored by entrepreneurs who like to count their chickens before they hatch.

inner-directed, *adj.* New-Age-Speak for people with get-up-and-go. All entrepreneurs are inner-directed; sometimes the direction turns inward to their wallets.

intrapreneur, *n.* entrepreneur working within the corporate setting. (No, it is *not* an oxymoronic definition.)

IPO, *n.* Initial Public Offering. The entrepreneurial equivalent of a garage sale.

Jobs and Wozniak, *n.* the Hewlett and Packard of the 1980s.

mega-, *prefix.* Used to describe anything large. As in megatrends, mega-generation (i.e., Baby-Boomers), megabucks.

micro-, *prefix*. Describes anything small and expensive. As in microcomputer, microbusiness. (If transistor radios had been invented in 1982, they would have been called microradios.)

OPM, *n*. Other People's Money. The best kind of capital.

PMA, *n*. Positive Mental Attitude. An attribute of all entrepreneurial types. Not to be confused with PMS, which female entrepreneurs sometimes also have.

risk, *n*. unstated mantra of every entrepreneur; the element that all entrepreneurs laugh in the face of. Also used as verb and in combination with other words: *risk*-taker (high compliment); *risk*-taking (average day at the office); and high-*risk* (perfect job description).

ROI, *n*. Return On Investment. The bottom line for venture capitalists.

Route 128, *n*. a Golden Strip outside Boston, Massachussetts.

seed money, *n*. little dollars out of which big enterprises grow.

Silicon Valley, *n*. the Promised Land of Bilk and Money.

skunkworks, *n*. in large companies, the repository of entrepreneurial types, or "skunks," who work away at seemingly impossible product innovations.

spreadsheet, *n*. essential software tool for entrepreneurs estimating start-up costs.

start-up, *n*. initial phase of an enterprise or venture. Not to be confused with upstarts, who frequently start start-ups.

sweat equity, *n*. sleepless nights and endless days that sometimes pay off in big bucks when the entrepreneur goes public.

tender offer, *n*. romantic bid by larger company to make beautiful music with your enterprise.

time-based, *adj*. derogatory term for the 9-to-5 world entrepreneurs leave behind. As in "What I do isn't really time-based."

unexercised shares, *n*. flabby portion of entrepreneur's prideful stake in company. Often target of ex-wife's acquisition strategy.

venture capital, *n*. funds offered by venturesome types who invest early in fledgling companies in exchange for a stake after going public. Or, the stuff that makes the entrepreneurial world go 'round.

window, *n*. short period of time when entrepreneur has access to venture capital, new markets, or other goodies.

ENTREVIEW

Charles Lindbergh Barr of Fleabag Express

Deregulation of the airline industry several years ago caused a flurry of excitement in the entrepreneurial world as small carriers began to spring up in all parts of the country. Sir Freddie Laker, who later succumbed to bankruptcy, became a role model for dozens of young enterprising types who wanted to own their own airlines. Charles Lindbergh Barr, one of the most successful of the new crop of aviatrepreneurs, agreed to speak to our Entrechic reporter. In just four years, he and his partners have built Fleabag Express into one of the largest "alternative" airline carriers offering "no-thrills" flights between major U.S. cities.

Entrechic: *How exactly did you hit upon the concept of "no frills or thrills" flights?*
Barr: The "no-frills" part was easy. We began to notice that Americans were buying more generic brands of coffee, toilet paper, and other products. From there, it was a short step to realizing that the public really didn't need or want all the airline extras, like in-flight meals, movies, or bathrooms.

EC: *How interesting. We now see how the generic tie-in explains the design look of your airplanes.*
Barr: Yes. We were delighted when our designer decided to go with the concept of the black and white generic food can. The stark white with the few black lines on it really distinguishes our aircraft. And, of course, there's a touch of whimsy in the supermarket computer code that's on the rear half of each jet.

EC: *In keeping with the canned food concept, was it long before that overall idea began to influence the design of the interior of the planes?*
Barr: No, it was just a matter of months, really. After we began eliminating frills, we saw how much the public would put up with to save a few bucks. That's when we hit on what we like to call in-house our "happy sardines" policy. We removed the seats of the aircraft and saw that we could get twice as many people in that way. And, since people were no longer on a level to see out the windows anyway, we eliminated them, too. That's where the "no thrills" part comes in. Windowless airplanes require a lot less maintenance, and our pilots no longer feel any urge to comment on the sights below.

EC: Well, all entrepreneurs out there looking for cost-cutting strategies could certainly take a page from your book, or a label from your can, ha ha. You mentioned your pilots. Is there any truth to the rumor that your human resources department goes to Brazil annually to recruit former Luftwaffe personnel?

Barr: No! Actually, I think I know how that rumor got started. We aim a lot of our advertising at Baby-Boomers, and in one radio spot we made the mistake of using that old rock song, "Snoopy and the Red Baron," as background music. Now, I don't want to point any fingers, but I do think that the big airlines have kind of encouraged the rumors that we have inferior pilots. It's not fair, but I suppose all is fair in love and fare wars.

3

THE DOWNSIDE OF THE ENTREPRENEURIAL EXISTENCE

WARNING: The federal government has determined that some of the pessimistic prose in this chapter could be dangerous to your entrepreneurial aspirations. When read to laboratory rats who were planning to start up their own testing ventures, 60 percent chose to remain with the parent lab. If your risk-taking ability is not strong enough to withstand access to negative feedback, consider skipping this chapter.

You might be asking yourself at this point, "If entrepreneurial chic is all it's cracked up to be, how come there are still people working for AT&T? How come we shop in big supermarkets instead of Mom and Pop ventures? Why do big corporations own half the world?"

Good questions. The simple truth is that not everybody has the Right Stuff to become an entrepreneur. Good entrepreneurs are like ballet dancers or acrobats, who make everything look easy. There is a lot of work involved in state-of-the-art entrepreneuring, and it's not for wimps or ordinary people who need to know where their next meal is coming from or whether or not they can keep their house until the end of the year. Sure, the lifestyles of the rich and entre-chic are impressive. But it takes a while—sometimes three months, sometimes three years—to get to the point where you can really relax and buy yourself a nice jet or yacht. In the meantime, it's work, work, work.

THE ENTREPRENEURIAL WORKOUT: SWEAT EQUITY

Unless you've developed the technology to clone Steven Spielberg and the venture capitalists are beating a path to your door, chances are the greatest asset you have to offer in the entrepreneurial world is an ability to work a 20-hour day. Savvy venturers who invest time and energy in lieu of big bucks build "sweat equity" in an enterprise. The very ease with which we speak of sweat equity shows the great strides toward female and animal liberation our society has taken in the last three decades. If entrepreneurial fever had hit in the 1950s, only horses would have produced sweat equity. Men would have built "perspiration equity," and women would have worked for "glow equity."

The exertion involved in building sweat equity slowly takes its toll, even on entrepreneurs in the best physical and mental shape. It's the business equivalent of an aerobics workout, and the most entrechic among us learn very early to "go for the burn." The following downside exercises will help you build good sweat equity or go insane within the first year of your start-up:

Spreadsheet sway. Place head in front of video spreadsheet. Move neck slowly back and forth to read columns. Repeat as necessary.

Put-in push-ups. Flex finger joints up and down on computer keyboard while inputting. Perform at least four times a day.

Touchtone touch. Bring arm from center of chest down to touch phone for each number. Repeat as long as necessary. (Don't cheat by using a phone with a two-digit memory code.)

Fast-food reach. Place styrofoam container with cheeseburger on left rear corner of desk. Stretch right arm out to retrieve. Repeat with soft drink on opposite side of desk, reaching with the left arm.

Coffee guzzle. Tip head and desk chair slightly backward, bring coffee to lips. Repeat often, taking care to arch the back.

Head/phone grip. Pick up phone and cradle it with neck muscle next to head. Every five minutes, switch sides. Exercise should last at least five hours a day.

Perplexed pace. Clasp hands on either side of head, walk swiftly back and forth. Groan on every fourth pass.

Seven-hour sit. Place buttocks in nonergonomically designed chair. When discomfort becomes unbearable, slowly lift one cheek, then the other. Repeat every fifteen minutes.

Audit rush. Run to file cabinet. Pick out ten pounds of files. Put them down. Run to window or up basement stairs to see if accountant or IRS auditor is on the way. Run back. Repeat once or twice a year.

Post office dash. Nervously watch clock. Prepare or have prepared important document upon which rides entire future of your company. Leave office at 4:57 with said document in hand. Attempt to get to post office before it closes. Perform daily if possible, or at least three times a week.

All-night worry. Lying in prone position, think about mounting debt. Sit up. Lie back down. Turn from side to side. Perform only at night, for five to eight hours.

Pulverize the partner. Pick up letter opener. Crawl on floor to position behind partner's desk. Leap up with grimace on face. Wrestle with partner, if desired, or run around office facility brandishing letter opener. If partnerless, use employee or close relative as target. A good exercise to rid oneself of excess stress.

Basement climb. Descend stairs to start-up operation. Ascend 16 hours later. Repeat daily.

Garage door lift. Lift door of start-up facility. Check weather conditions and time of day. Push door back down. Perform often, unless in danger of having a zoning violation discovered.

THE PSYCHOLOGICAL DOWNSIDE: WHAT THE SHRINKS SAY

Entrepreneurship entails a lot of positive character traits: ambition, self-confidence, a sense of independence, and a positive attitude, to name a few. On the flip side of all these attributes, however, lie a bunch of reputedly negative aspects to the entrepreneurial profile. Some doom-saying psychologists, the types who prefer to think the glass is half empty rather than half full, have begun to criticize the forceful entrepreneurial personality; they are now trying to develop therapy strategies for the most common psychological problems entrepreneurs face.

According to a recent study released in *Venture* magazine, the average entrepreneur is a somewhat paranoiac personality. They often felt persecuted as a regular employee and became motivated to wreak revenge on "the boss" by leaving and starting an independent enterprise. They have an almost unhealthy disdain for authority and an eagerness to exaggerate those feelings of exploitation in order to rationalize quitting a good job. Once out in the world, they are liable to have trouble with anyone who doesn't share their single-minded obsession with the venture at hand, including a spouse, employees, and bank officials.

These security-minded shrinks seem to think the hunger for power makes an entrepreneur a difficult person to live with or work for. If you have fully embraced the entrechic way of life, your missionarylike zeal just might be blinding you from the way others assess your personality. This does not mean that you should adjust your personality in any way. On the contrary, you'll be a dismal failure if you try to act like one of the ordinary drones who go to work from 9 to 5 and take the kids to the beach on weekends. But you should be aware of the prejudice and sense of sour grapes among many sectors of society—including the world of professional psychology—that will always influence detractors to misinterpret your personality traits.

To further this awareness, consult the following chart, which explains how your own assessment of your best features becomes warped by those outside the entrepreneurial world.

Entrepreneurial Characteristics

How you see yourself	How the rest of the world sees you
enthusiastic	maniacal
ambitious	cutthroat
take-charge	dictatorial
independent-minded	alienated
self-confident	narcissistic
risk-taking	suicidal
directed	obsessive
hard-working	repressive
aggressive	power-hungry
savvy	greedy

Who Me, Paranoid? Who Me, Hostile?

The following short test will help you determine your general level of entrepreneurial bile. Complete the sentences below.

1. Every boss I ever worked for was
   A. very nice and supportive.
   B. stupid.
   C. out to get me.
   D. a Nazi war criminal.
2. My fellow employees over the years have been
   A. interesting people.
   B. idiots and charlatans.
   C. snakes in the grass.
   D. Benedict Arnolds.
3. When I worked for someone else, my ideas
   A. always received the proper recognition.
   B. were ignored.
   C. were ridiculed.
   D. were stolen by Machiavellian nincompoops.
4. I became or want to become an entrepreneur
   A. to make lots of money.
   B. to make the world a better place.
   C. to show I'm smarter than everybody else.
   D. to eventually get rich enough to buy out my old company and fire everyone.

Scoring: All C and D answers indicate a high level of entrepreneurial paranoia and zeal. If you answered A or B to more than one question, reconsider your entrepreneurial ambitions. You're too complacent to become a revered risk-taker.

SHRINK SHORTHAND FOR THE ENTREPRENEURIAL PERSONALITY

Psychiatrists and psychologists have obviously never learned Mom's advice that "if you can't say something good about a person, don't say anything." Through the years, they've been pointing out what they see as defects in the entrepreneurial personality.

Unresolved sibling rivalry. Psychologists refuse to believe the simple truth that entrepreneurs are more brilliant than their coworkers and bosses, and hence must leave those people behind in their quest for success. Instead, many shrinks will try to tell you that the competitive entrepreneurial personality arises from unresolved childhood conflicts with brothers and sisters. This interpretation is patently ridiculous. All entrepreneurs know from the age of three that they are better than their siblings anyway, so why would there possibly be conflict?

Insecurity. Many analysts interpret the entrepreneur's ambition as a cry for attention that really stems from insecurity rather than confidence. Let's be fair here. Just because a guy wants to be a millionaire doesn't necessarily mean he craves attention. Look at Howard Hughes.

Possessiveness. The entrepreneur is saying, "Mine, mine, mine!" according to some shrinks, who see entrechic types as control freaks who like to create their very own microcosm of the universe. These psychologists charge that entrepreneurs have problems delegating authority and tend to interfere in every aspect of their growing enterprises. To this, we say: Delegation is for wimps. It's healthy to have a proprietary interest in something you've built from scratch. Doesn't God still interfere with things once in a while?

Entrepreneurs Speak Out: The Entrerap Group

The pressures of the lone-track life cause some entrepreneurs to seek the company of sympathetic peers. Three years ago, Boston fiberoptics entrepreneur Sid Ventureman formed a rap group for people like himself who wanted to talk about the nitty-gritty, emotional side of entrepreneurship. The first advertisement for the discussion group in the local *Risk Gazette* brought over 300 responses. Since then, Sid has franchised Entrerap in 30 cities. Group members pay dues and pledge small shares company equity to each other. They meet once a week to discuss their feelings about the downside of the entrepreneurial experience.

Sid was kind enough to allow us to sit in on an Entrerap group with six members. He still leads a few groups himself, this one among them. In the group are Steve, 38, owner of a national fast-food crudité and dip franchise; Karen, 29, founder of a software concern; Ralph, 42, owner of a human resources consulting firm; Abdul, 32, who imports Oriental rugs for Mercedes sedans; Shirley, 37, who started up a gourmet shop that now markets its foods nationally; and, Kirk, 22, whose new microcomputer was just named the official portable computer of the 1988 Olympics.

Sid: Hi, everybody. I hope you don't mind our visitor. We'll start the meeting as usual—with the Riskaholics Anonymous prayer:

Innovative spirit, grant us the ability to change the world, and the patience to accept that it might take over ten years to earn more than a million. And grant us the wisdom to know the difference between a good risk and a crazy concept. Amen.

Well, how has everyone's week been? Has it been downside or upside?
Ralph: Decidedly downside for me. My wife up and left me.
Karen: Poor baby. How did it happen? Did you have any idea it was coming?
Ralph: Well, we hadn't had much time to talk lately, I have to admit. I have this new account with IBM, and I was spending a lot of time at the office working on it. I even had to ask my secretary to turn away Susan's calls. For Christ's sake, this was a really big one. *IBM* wanted my consulting firm to totally reorganize their human resources department!
Steve: Wow, that *is* a biggie. I'm surprised your wife didn't understand. You've been married twenty years. Why did it suddenly start to bug her now?
Ralph: Well, I've only had the company for five years. But I just don't know. She left me a real long note, and in it she said she wished I'd had an affair or something, that she could cope with that. But she said she couldn't stand it that the "other woman" was a consulting firm. She said she couldn't compete with the allure of work.
Sid: Ralph, I don't want to sound judgmental, but I have a gut feeling that you should have given that lady better access to you.
Kirk: I know I'm too young to know about marriage, but this reminds me of the funny way my parents used to act when I was in the process of getting the venture capital for my computer firm. Like, you know, they resented competing with my work for my attention. They said they could cope with it better if I was just a fourteen-year-old with a drug problem or something normal like that. But we patched it up later, after my company went public on my eighteenth birthday. Then I took a week off and the whole family flew to Paris on the Concorde. Suddenly, we were close again.

Shirley: Hey, that's not a bad idea. How about taking your wife on a vacation for a while, just the two of you? Before that case of frozen crepes fell on my husband, he and I used to get away all the time.

Abdul: Shirley, what's wrong with you? Ralph has a big new account, remember? How about a present? That doesn't take as much time. Plus, maybe she can come have dinner with you at the office or something.

Ralph: Those are good suggestions, but Susan's not much of a risk-taker. Her friends all have these nine-to-five husbands who come home for dinner. She would just think it's weird to meet me at the office. But I could try the present. It's just that she seems pretty determined to divorce me.

Karen: You should at least try it. That's what happened with me. My husband got me a personal computer as a present after a terrible argument. Instead of leaving him, I ended up designing software! Get her a hobby or her own company. Then it won't matter if you don't see each other. She'll be so busy, she won't care either. I tell you, when I do see my husband every once in a while—he runs his own airline—it's just like we're newlyweds again.

Abdul: May I make a suggestion? I think what Karen's saying is right on the mark. But don't forget to put some romance in it. Give her a computer, sure, but maybe tape a diamond to the disk-drive door or something like that.

Kirk: You know, Abdul, I really resent what you're saying. Are you suggesting that state-of-the-art computers aren't romantic products?

Abdul: I hear you, Kirk. It's just that sometimes older consumers don't associate bits and bytes with good sexual feelings. It's not just your product. I hate to admit it, but a lot of women probably would rather have a diamond ring than an Oriental rug, which, incidentally, is a much better investment.

Shirley: Will you two stop talking about your ventures? You know this group is supposed to be about the *emotional* side of entrepreneurship.

Steve: Oh, come off it, Shirley. You know all of us can't go more than about fifteen minutes without mentioning our life's work.

Sid: Yes, that is unfortunately all too true. And my beeper has just gone off. Something must be screwed up over at Opti-Scan. Can we continue this discussion about Ralph's tragedy at our next meeting?

Ralph: Uh, I can't make the meeting next week. I'm flying out to San Francisco to see a client. But if any of you want to give me more advice, leave messages with my secretary. I'll be calling in.

"There are moments in history which are significant, and to be a part of one of those moments is an incredible experience. In other words, there are more important things than cooking in your own kitchen."

Apple Computer co-founder Steven Jobs, talking about the long work hours associated with the entrepreneurial lifestyle.

DOWNSIDE DISEASES: THE PREDISPOSITION OF THE ENTREPRENEUR

No discussion of the negative aspects of entrechic would be complete without at least a nod toward the physiological ramifications of mega-ambitions. Some doctors contend that a meteoric rise in the business world leads to diseases of the body and mind. While we are unsure that working 95-hour weeks has any effects on a person's health, some entrepreneurs have been known to succumb to disease now and then. Be on the lookout for the following cripplers that can severely diminish the enjoyment of your capital gains.

HEART ATTACK

Dropping dead of a heart attack is every male entrepreneur's worst fear. Not only does it put a crimp in future plans, but it's so clichéd! It's also aggravating that your wife will get the satisfaction of saying, "I kept telling him if he kept on that way, he'd have a heart attack." Of course, there are things you can do to try to avoid such a demise, but those all have their downside, too. Eating a low-cholesterol, low-fat diet makes it difficult to order in fast food during all-nighters at the office. And modifying the aggressive behavior some physicians call Type A could spell the downfall of your entrepreneurial verve. Some entrepreneurs took to jogging to condition their bodies, but the death of Jim Fixx calls into question the "run for your life" strategy.

OBESITY

Restaurateurs or food entrepreneurs become particularly vulnerable to the side effects of superfluous calories. So do entrepreneurs who put in long hours at the desk and can't find the time to hit the gym. If you seek the higher entrechic echelons, you cannot afford this chronic illness, since excess chubbiness will make you look less appealing in photographs and on television (*especially* on the tube, where even Bobby Sands looked a bit hefty).

ULCERS AND GASTROINTESTINAL COMPLAINTS

Something's literally eating you, and the result is major holes in your digestive tract. It's not a good gut feeling. The ultimate cure is probably to sell your enterprise, but you can also hang on until you get famous enough to spell relief in Rolaids commercials.

DRUG ABUSE

With some entrepreneurs practicing creative financing deals centered on controlled substances, it's just a matter of time before some famous entrechic sex symbol will check into the Betty Ford Clinic to detoxify. Be wary if you're suddenly developing an addiction to No-Doz or Sominex. You know it won't stop there.

ENTRE-NOUS: AN ADVICE COLUMN BY AUNTIE PRENOOR

Dear Auntie Prenoor,

I'm a 33-year-old man who's been happily married for six years. But recently my wife and I have been arguing almost every day about something I just don't understand. Ever since I got out of college, I've had a good job with the government. Over the years, I've risen through the ranks so that I'm making a pretty good salary. I even get on TV once in a while when there's a crisis and I'm a spokesperson.

My wife isn't happy. She says her friends at aerobics class laugh when she tells them I still work 9 to 5. Her best friend Debbie's husband started a software company that just went public. Sally's live-in friend Larry started a restaurant that got a 3,000-word writeup in Esquire. My wife has started begging me to do anything but work for the government.

''It's so dull,'' she whines. Now she wants me to sell our boat and take a second mortgage on the house just to get the thrill of risk all her friends keep talking about. But I don't have an idea in the world about starting a business. Last Christmas she bought me subscriptions to Venture and Inc. She even says she's toying with selling her engagement ring to buy a Mary Kay cosmetics franchise.

I love my wife, but what can I do? I'm too set in my ways to become an entrepreneur. Auntie, can this marriage be saved?

Security Freak in Alexandria

Dear Security Freak,
Wake up and smell the silicon chips. While I can understand some mild hesitation on your part, what you have been putting your poor wife through is inexcusable. A 33-year-old man has no business enjoying government work. Why, most normal husbands have started at least three companies by the time they're 32, and their wives have enjoyed the perks of press attention.

Since your wife is obviously a stifled risk-taker, I say go for it! Let her pick what type of enterprise you start. Remember, the chances are that the strains of starting a new enterprise will break up your marriage anyway, so why worry? Get capital and get going!

Dear Auntie Prenoor,
I'm a middle-aged entrepreneur with a profitable family firm. I never got to finish college myself, so I really wanted Junior to get his degree. I sent him to the best Ivy League college he could get into, and I never made him work during school. He graduated at the bottom of his class last year, and my wife and I tried to be proud even though we wish he would have worked a little harder.

Now here's my problem. Naturally, I took Junior into the firm when he graduated. Then I started realizing why he didn't do so well in school. Junior's a blithering idiot. This is a big problem for me, because he messes everything up and all my employees hate me because he sits around doing hardly

anything all day long. I haven't wanted
to mention this to my wife, because I
think he takes after her side of the
family—not a savvy entrepreneur among
them.

What can I do? I was hoping to retire in ten years and leave the company
to Junior. Now I feel like I might as
well burn the place down.

The Brains Stop Here

Dear Brains,

*Obviously, Junior needs help. If you know
a clergyman who's also had experience in venture capital funds, have him talk to your son. If
no such person is available, you might want to
consider sending Junior to entrepreneur camp.
These types of "outward bound" experiences can
build character and change an unmotivated
college graduate into an inner-directed dy-
namo.*

*But a word of caution here: As you seem to
already suspect, Junior might just not have
what it takes. If this is the case, you're going to
have to deposit your son in some harmless department in your company, like public relations
or personnel. Give him a secretary and then forget about him. (Also cut him out of your will if
possible.) Then set about grooming another
child or scouring the neighborhood for street-
wise entrepreneurial material. Start dining out
more at ethnic restaurants as part of your scout-
ing activities. Remember, studies show that im-
migrants show a particular propensity for risk-
taking. You might just need new blood for the
company, and adoption would give you the
peace of mind you'll need to retire.*

Thanks for writing. I hope your sad story will give other entrepreneurs pause to think before they marry people from nonentrepreneurial gene pools.

Dear Auntie Prenoor,
My name is Rachel and I'm eight years old. There's this man who comes to our house sometimes late at night and my Mommy says he is my Daddy. She says he can't see me too much because of his "damn company." Does that mean he has lots of people visit him, like when Mommy and me have company?
None of my friends believe I have a Daddy. But my teacher told me she saw a blurb on him in The Wall Street Journal. What's a blurb? How can I get the other kids to believe I have a Daddy?

Confused Kid

Dear Confused,
A company is a place where people go to work. Your Daddy is busy making things good for you and your Mommy. When Daddy sells that company, you're going to have lots of wonderful things. He'll probably be able to buy you ten Cabbage Patch dolls. A blurb, honey, is a nice little poem all about how great your Daddy is. But good daddies aren't satisfied with blurbs. They want a feature-length article. Someday, when you're older and need to bring something in to current affairs class, won't you be proud if you can bring in a whole long article on Daddy? Sure you will.

So don't pay attention to the other kids. They might get to see their daddies, but who cares? Nobody wants a Daddy who's a loser, anyway.

Dear Auntie Prenoor,

Please help me. I think my husband is a start-up addict. I married Gus because he had a lot of drive, and over the years he's provided well for me and our four children. But lately he has avoided all involvement in his home life because he has started up 30 ventures in the last 18 months! These are all in addition to his regular job as an investment banker.

And the enterprises aren't even all in the same field or with the same people. He has started up high-tech companies, restaurants, cleaning services, ice cream shops, and travel agencies. Altogether, he has 52 partners. Our house now has ten phone lines and eight answering machines. Two software companies, one computer company, and a biotech place making microbes designed to clean kitty litter are all sharing our basement. You can imagine the extra coffee expenses!

Gus used to be reasonable, but every time I mention the constraints all these start-ups have placed on our lives (not to mention our savings account), he blows up. He tells me I don't understand that this is the 1980s. He says we'll really kick ourselves if we don't cash in on this entrepreneurial economy.

Auntie, I don't want to crush his dreams, but I need my basement back. I haven't been able to do a load of laundry in peace for six months. And the mailman who used to be so nice is now throwing a six-pound packet of mail at our screen door every day. What can I do?

Fed-up with Start-ups

Dear Fed-up,

First, let me congratulate you on being married to such a gem. It's not every wife who can so proudly say her husband is riding the crest of a megatrend. However, I did contact Dr. Otto Sprout of the Center for Entrepreneurial Psychology, who told me that the recommended limit for start-ups per person was 22. With this in mind, see if you can get Gus to consolidate a few of his ventures. I see no reason, for example, why the two software companies can't merge if the partners are agreeable.

Now there's the matter of your household problems. I can understand your frustration, and I recommend that you and Gus and the four children move out of the house to a small garden apartment for a while. That way, the frenzied start-up atmosphere won't affect family life. If Gus fails to agree to this, you must really put your foot down. Send out your laundry and insist that he rent a postal box so your mailman won't sue for hernia surgery expenses.

ENTREVIEW

Michelangelo Davis of ARTV,
a cable network featuring
live presentations of famous
paintings

The video revolution has spawned special cable channels geared toward narrow viewing audiences. One surprise has been the success of other media, such as music and art, in infiltrating the airwaves. When Michelangelo Davis, a former art history professor, founded ARTV in 1983, few critics thought it would survive. But survive it did, and, indeed, it has flourished. Fans of the cable channel say they much prefer seeing live tableaux of actors portraying famous masterpieces than going to museums to see the paintings themselves.

Entrechic: *How many paintings does your network "portray" per day?*
Davis: Let's see. We're on twenty-four hours a day, and each performance lasts about four minutes. That's approximately three hundred eighty paintings a day.

EC: *Wow! That's a lot more famous paintings than an average tourist could see in a year of traveling.*
Davis: Our channel is really a service that way. It expands people's knowledge of Western art while also giving them a good time.

EC: *But wouldn't it be easier and a little more accurate just to show the actual paintings for four minutes, rather than a bunch of actors in a set within a frame?*
Davis: Believe me, it would be easier. We wouldn't have the tremendous overhead costs of acting personnel and set designers. But we test-marketed that concept a couple of years ago and it was a terrible flop.

EC: *Why do you think it failed?*
Davis: As near as we can tell from our research, there just wasn't enough excitement in it. It reminded people too much of all those slides in college art classes. Our format with live actors is just the opposite. It fascinates TV viewers. They wait around to see if one of the actors will surreptitiously scratch an unmentionable body part. They argue about whether the woman playing Mona Lisa has the right smile.

EC: *This concept is a total departure from anything that's been done before. How did you come to develop it?*
Davis: It was really a Christmastime inspiration. Before the ACLU started going on the warpath, my small town in Connecticut used to mount a living crèche scene with actors and farm animals every holiday season. I thought, "Gee, we could do the same thing with famous masterpieces."

EC: *Speaking of animals, I would imagine they'd be difficult to control during the filming of a "painting."*
Davis: Murder! We only did one of those Edward Hicks "Peaceable Kingdom" paintings, and I said, "No more!" It took thirty-five takes to get it right, and the sheep and the lion did *not get along at all.*

EC: *What other special difficulties have you had over the years?*

Davis: Well, casting is particularly tricky. Not many people look like the models in old paintings. Our scouts scour the country looking for Rubenesque beauties, for example. The health and fitness craze makes it real hard to find women with bellies large enough to look good in a Renoir painting. And all the actresses are too tan! Sometimes we have to let them sit in a dark room for a couple of days to get that pasty look that lends historical authenticity. And you wouldn't believe how much trouble we have doing landscapes. We bought up a whole bunch of old MGM backdrops, but sometimes even with alterations they just don't work for artists like, say, Turner or Eakins.

EC: Are there paintings you'd like to attempt but can't?
Davis: For obvious reasons, we've never tackled the postwar expressionists. We're working on a deal right now with the Disney studios to see if we can do animated versions of some Jackson Pollocks and Robert Motherwells. I feel badly that modern art is underrepresented on the channel. But recently we mounted a rather nice production of Andy Warhol's Campbell soup cans.

EC: You are a former professor of art history at Yale. Does it bother you that some members of the art world have called ARTV a "sacrilege" and "the worst curse that ever could have befallen Western art?"
Davis: Those of us who believe that art is something to be enjoyed by the masses, and *not* the province of a few pointy-headed intellectuals, are accustomed to dealing with the snobbery of the critical establishment. And, if I may speak frankly, there is more than a bit of professional jealously involved in the negative reviews of our channel. Professors of art history don't usually make much money, let alone make the cover of *People* magazine, as I did recently.

EC: What's next on your entrepreneurial agenda? We've heard rumors that ARTV is about to expand.
Davis: Yes. Next month, SCULPTV makes its debut with depictions of famous sculpture throughout the world. It took a few years to develop because our makeup department was searching for a substance that would make the actors most resemble marble and other stone surfaces. Now we've found it. We might not be quite up to tackling Mount Rushmore yet, but you'll be able to see most of your favorite statues right in the privacy of your own home.

4

UPSCALING THE HEIGHTS OF ENTRECHIC: THE AFTER-HOURS LIFESTYLE

For some, entrepreneurship is an end in itself. They spend their days and nights contentedly working on new projects or drawing up business plans for future ventures. Not so for seekers of entrechic, who long for the upscale rewards that come along with phenomenal success. Should you be among those who adore power, money, and fame, you'll enjoy the later stages of entrepreneurship best when your company has gone public, you've franchised your retail store, or you've sold your small firm to a large conglomerate for a tidy sum. That's when you'll start accumulating all the toys that make the journey worthwile. In the meantime, before you cash in your chips, use this chapter to help you focus on ultimate material goals.

Remember, leading-edge entrepreneurs use their personal discretionary funds in ways that distinguish them from the old-style "mink coat and cigar" business set. They show off affluence and success more subtly yet more extravagantly than the organization men of the 1950s. Entrepreneurs wouldn't be caught dead in a Cadillac, for example. And they wouldn't necessarily pay off the house mortgage as a symbol of "making it." But a young self-made type in pursuit of entrechic might not think twice about spending $100,000 on a two-year trek through the Himalayas. Entrepreneurial successes spend the same amount of time and energy seeking unique, risky lifestyles as they did in the start-up stages of their enterprises.

Two unspoken yet very clear rules govern all entrepreneurs' search for happiness. First, they want their possessions to reflect a personal style, an individual *je ne sais quoi*. That's why trite mass-made American success symbols such as Cadillacs or mink coats don't entice the true entrepreneur. Second, entrepreneurs don't want *everything* in their life to be upscale. In fact, a sort of reverse chic forms the fabric of the entrepreneurial existence. Some things are so downscale that they become upscale. There's no contradiction in having a $1000 tape deck in a beat-up Toyota, or $20,000 worth of computer equipment sitting on the floor of an empty house filled with old Snickers wrappers. It's just an entrepreneurial style of decorating that helps the very entrechic rationalize their enormous wealth.

ENTREMOBILES: YOU ARE WHAT YOU DRIVE

Because many of the social rules of the entrechic lifestyle emanate from car-infested California, the automobile figures prominently in any venturer's image. Your mode of transportation must be either definitely upscale or so downscale that it's upscale—say, a 1972 bashed-up Chevy Nova. Other downscale but chic junkers include old VW vans or bugs, any kind of ancient Honda, old Dodge Darts, and very old Volvos.

These older vehicles will suffice until you make your first three million bucks or so. Keep at least one of them until a few magazine reporters drop by. Then they'll write about how you are so unaffected by fame that you still drive a ten-year-old car. As soon as your first round of interviews are over, though, junk the junkers and get yourself one or several of the acceptable *nouveau riche* models.

Tire-Kicking Tips

Ironically, even though entrepreneurs are credited with reviving the American economy, they *never* drive American cars. Whatever choice you make, remember that it should be foreign and over $25,000.

SPORTS CARS

Think turbo. The more cylinders, the better. Twelve is optimum, because speed engenders risk. The car should look like no one over four feet tall could possibly fit behind the steering wheel. The Porsche 928S is the most popular, although it and similar models seem a bit trite these days. Innovative types seek the Jaguar S-type, the Maserati Quattroporte, the Ferrari Boxer or Testa Rossa, the Lamborghini Countach, and the Lotus Turbo Esprit. In his heart, every male entrepreneur wants to look like James Bond or Magnum, P.I.

SEDANS

Mercedes is still standard issue for folks who have suddenly made it. Get one or more for those times when you need a back seat. Another entrechic family car is the dependable BMW. Deutschland has it *über Alles* when it comes to wealth on wheels, but some entrepreneurs who hit it big do choose an outrageously expensive Rolls Royce or Aston Martin. Yet the Britmobiles seem rather gauche, and an entrepreneur in a Silver Spirit risks being mistaken for a Hollywood agent rather than a savior of the American economic system.

RECREATIONAL VEHICLES

Many outdoorsy risk-takers like to keep four-wheel-drive jeeps or micro pickup trucks at their mountain hideaways. The ultimate upscale jeep is from Mercedes. It costs about $28,000, but who said class is cheap? Drive it to the office to look your macho best.

STANDARD ACCESSORIES FOR THE ENTREMOBILE

Sun roof, computer (to run engine), cellular mobile phone unit, leather seats, tape deck and radio worth over $2000.

Vanity Plates: Cute or Déclassé?

A debate rages in entrechic circles about vanity plates. Objections to individualized tags range from paranoia about kidnapping and theft to disdain for the "uncoolness" of announcing oneself to the world via a back bumper. People who speak in favor of the metal epithets say it's just good clean road fun. If you feel the urge to put in-jokes on a set of license plates, remember these rules:

1. Avoid sickening nicknames like Bunny, Kiki, or Honey. They'll make you look like you work for Mary Kay cosmetics.
2. Avoid sexy come-ons like Stud, Hunk, or Foxy. An entrepreneur's charisma should emerge in a subtler fashion.
3. Use coded references to your enterprise such as abbreviations of company slogans or products, but *never* refer to money or profits on a license plate. It's totally tasteless.

THE PLACE TO PARK YOUR CAR: HOME

Entrepreneurs are not ostentatious when it comes to their dwellings. They eventually like to own a main residence or vacation house that's worth a couple of hundred thousand, but the homes needn't be flashy. A calculated casualness imbues entrechic home-ownership, probably because true visionaries don't spend as much time at home as they do at work. As with cars, entredwellings can even be fashionably downscale, especially in the first few years of entrepreneurial life. Hence the large number of start-up venturers occupying beach cottages, houseboats, old lofts, and even house trailers. Deals are not cut or uncut because of what a person's house looks like. Your own tastes and family size should determine furnishings. For the very early stages of start-up, it pays to have a nice garage or basement, too.

Only one hard and fast rule applies to entrepreneurial home-ownership, and that has to do with electronic gadgets. All entrepreneurs, whether involved in high-tech or low-tech operations, cannot resist technological toys for their living spaces. They will often take risks on buying unusual and expensive computers or video equipment that's not yet in the mainstream marketplace. An entrechic home should contain several computers plus modems to provide linkage with the outside world, two or more VCRs, at least two state-of-the-art stereo systems, and a gadget-filled gourmet kitchen. Optional items include a sauna or jacuzzi, satellite disk, intercom system, pet robot, alarm system (to protect the state-of-the-art equipment), and special avocational living spaces such as exercise studios, greenhouses with hydroponic systems, or photographic darkrooms.

The Hot Spots: Entrepreneurial Communities in the U.S.A.

Location is a much more important consideration than actual housing stock. As an ordinary entrepreneur, you can live almost anywhere. But as one seeking the ultimate in entrechic, you'll want to scout out the most desirable entreclaves. Living in an officially designated entrepreneurial community increases networking possibilities for future ventures and makes things easier when those magazines come to do photo sessions.

When rating various locations, check out the following aspects of the lifestyle.

ACCESS TO BRAINPOWER

Most trendy entrepreneurial living centers cluster around prominent universities, which provide highly skilled personnel and special research and development facilities. For example, Silicon Valley in California benefits from a steady influx of Stanford and Berkeley graduates.

UPSIDE SURROUNDINGS

Few aspiring entrepreneurs hanker after substandard housing or dangerous neighborhoods. Despite all the talk about urban "enterprise zones," you'll find those in the know in safe suburban locales or gentrified neighborhoods.

ACCESS TO OTHER MOVERS AND SHAKERS

No man is an island, not even an entrepreneur. But entrepreneurship *is* isolating, so founders of companies tend to look for other start-up and ongoing enterprises that have located in the same area. Plus, when geniuses are fired or leave an established company, they usually start a new one around the corner. This is how entrepreneurial communities are birthed.

GOOD LAWYERS AND MARRIAGE COUNSELORS

Because entrepreneurs have trouble remembering their home address and their kids' names, they often require the special services of marital consultants.

RECREATIONAL POSSIBILITIES

Access to risk-taking sports (mountain climbing, hang gliding, scuba diving) is a must, in addition to good facilities for more mundane activities that are good for cutting deals, such as tennis, squash, and golf.

LOW TAXES

In the race for entrepreneurial start-ups, states with no or low income taxes and reasonable property taxes are beginning to win. Of course, sometimes entrepreneurs locate in more famous, high-tax communities just so they'll have something to complain about.

NAMEABILITY

It is good if the area is located in a valley so that journalists can dub it with some cute name. Silicon Valley in California and Polymer Valley in Ohio are two good examples. You know your industry has really made it when one of its components is used as an adjective.

RISK-TAKING AVOCATIONS FOR THE ENTRECHIC SET

Entrepreneurs work hard and play hard. In the rare instances when they unwind or go on vacation, they're likely to seek unusual experiences to strengthen their risk-taking abilities. While you might want to take up golf, racquetball, or tennis as an excellent entrée into the world of networking and deal-cutting, choose from among the following dangerous avocations for the rest of your spare time:

Skydiving, scuba diving, fixed-object parachuting (base jumping), abalone hunting, hot air ballooning, windsurfing, treasure hunting, hang gliding, triathlon training, ultralight aircraft, survival training, rock climbing, cliff diving, mountain climbing, ski jumping, Himalayan trekking, race car driving.

Jets and Yachts: Optional Accessories

Those old-fashioned symbols of corporate success, the company jet and yacht, have made a successful transition to the entrepreneurial scene. A cute little jet plane represents a much hipper image than an old-wave type seagoing yacht, but both set the successful entrepreneur apart from the rest of the 9-to-5 drones who must travel by more ordinary means.

If you do make it into the tax bracket enabling the purchase of mega-toys, keep in mind the following guidelines:

1. *Always customize.* A ship or an aircraft is seldom impressive unless you take the time to give it a personal touch. The bathrooms, for example, should exude a sense of wealth and hedonism. In fact, if you buy a jet, don't hesitate to equip it with things you might not have in your house. You'll probably spend more time in the jet, anyway.

2. *Always take the helm.* You'll be considered a wimp if you can't pilot your own ship or fly your own plane. And take care to get publicity shots of you at the control board.

Dress for Access: The Entrepreneurial Wardrobe

In the freewheeling entrepreneurial community, clothes do *not* make the man or woman. You may want to own one pinstriped number for forays into the "straight" business environments of lawyers, venture capitalists, and bankers. But you can spend the rest of your time in the type of casual, rumpled clothes that hold up well during 14-hour days. Everything you wear should be at least three years old, if not older. Naturally, retail or restaurant entrepreneurs might want to appear a little more snazzy than those who hibernate behind a desk or computer terminal. Here are some of the staples of an entrechic wardrobe:

Men: Corduroy pants and jacket, plaid cotton or flannel shirts.
Women: Same as above.

ENTREPRENEWS: PLAYING THE PUBLICITY GAME

You might make millions of dollars and employ hundreds of people, but you haven't reached the pinnacle of entrechic until you've become a household word. And the only way to raise your visibility is to get your face plastered across newspapers and onto magazine covers. With a large enough enterprise, your public relations department can take over the onerous task of making you appear to be a hot personality. But before that time, the individual entrepreneur must spend some time paying attention to press opportunities. Here are various progress levels for the publicity-conscious.

PARTY TALK

During the hectic phase of brainstorming and start-up, don't forget to take time off to talk up your enterprise at parties and other public affairs. Really lay it on thick. When people make polite inquiries, it's never out of line to say something like "We're developing a new concept in artificial intelligence," even if you are in reality opening up a sock store. This pre-publicity technique will sow the seeds for later recognition and adulation.

ALUMNI BULLETINS

Surprisingly, many people forget about these free grapevines. Desperate for news, alumni publications will print *anything*. Send them a note saying "Fred Harrowsmith ('69) has founded PhoneUp-Now, a telecommunications company whose profits will eclipse those of AT&T by 1987." They'll print it because not even the editors of those bulletins look at the copy. If you're extremely lucky, a former classmate who works for *The Wall Street Journal* will get stuck in her apartment elevator with only the alumni rag to read. Bingo!

ENTRY-LEVEL QUOTES

Always volunteer to be interviewed about other people's companies or at the scene of accidents and fires. Reporters like to characterize interviewees in ways that can be helpful to the publicity-seeker. Example: " 'She really was a nice old lady. What a horrible way to die,' said neighbor Fred Harrowsmith, president and CEO of PhoneUpNow, a telecommunications company that is offering keen competition to the likes of AT&T."

CULT MAG BLURBS

Once you have more than one employee, it won't be long before the entrepeneurial magazines begin sniffing you out. Send all press releases, spreadsheets, and venture capital offers to *Success!, Venture, Inc., In Business,* and *Entrepreneur.* Chances are they'll take the bait, because these cult publications for seekers of megabucks use hundreds of inspiring snippets about start-ups. If you don't hear from them in your first few months of operations, hire a high school kid to call their offices every day.

MAINSTREAM MAG BLURBS

The big time. This coverage could fall into your lap just because of a few appearances in the more specialized journals. Put on your best telephone-answering voice when *Fortune, Forbes,* or *Business Week* call, but don't exaggerate about your projected net or plans for growth, because these respectable magazines employ many fact-checkers and have a lot of contacts at huge corporations. You don't want to see something like this in print: " 'Fred Harrowsmith's company? Huh! I only just heard of it last week. PhoneUpNow probably has less than .003 percent market share,' said an AT&T spokesperson."

BUSINESS PAGE PLUG

When you reach the blurb section of a major newspaper's business pages or *The Wall Street Journal,* you're on your way to Studio 54 and a possible evening out with Warren Beatty or Diane Keaton.

It's imperative that your company do something that makes a nice little headline for the newspaper reporters, such as:

E.T., PhoneUpNow

Today, movie producer Steven Spielberg and Fred Harrowsmith, president of PhoneUpNow, a small communications concern in Poughkeepsie, New York, announced a new line of E.T. phones for office use. An AT&T spokesperson had no comment on the company's loss of the lucrative contract, which most industry insiders had thought would go to the larger telecommunications company.

BUSINESS PAGE FEATURE STORY

Get a haircut before the photographer comes around. Get the copy machine rolling and break out the Korbel if the paper's circulation is more than 500,000.

CULT MAG FEATURE STORY

While a cover story is best, any feature story with large, bold quotes and a picture of you standing in front of corporate headquarters is an excellent start on fame. Avoid the temptation to include your dog, personal computer, or spouse in the photo-taking session. It's already been done.

MAINSTREAM MAG FEATURE STORY

You might have to wait a long time for this one, but true entrechic will prevail. If your enterprise is humming along, take a few months off and volunteer to run the Olympics, Superbowl, or Presidential Inauguration. Events of this sort will bring high visibility and maybe even a few cover stories. ("Telecommunications magnate Fred Harrowsmith of PhoneUpNow made waves with the announcement of his sabbatical in order to emcee four beauty pageants this year . . . .") Sad to say, spectacular failure also attracts feature writers. No one wants to be the object of a "vulture" profile, but even stories dissecting your fabulous flop could land you a few talk-show appearances, a university teaching post, or a lucrative book contract.

CLIPPING SERVICE NIRVANA

Only a select few ever reach this highest rung of the publicity ladder. Entrepreneurs who employ someone full-time to keep track of their media presence and who appear in *New Yorker* cartoons serve as inspiring role models for all of us. Included in this lofty group are Steven Jobs, John Naisbitt, Peter Ueberroth, Donald Trump, and Fred Harrowsmith.

Interview Tips

Worried that instant fame will take you by surprise? Cut out this chart and keep it by your telephone at all times. It will give you instant topic areas for the various publications that might call when you hit it big.

Interview Tips

Publication	What you should talk about
Inc. *Venture* *Success*	concepts, capitalization, projected earnings, difficulty of start-up
People *Us*	your marriage, your divorce, your hobbies, your famous parents, your personal wealth, your movie star lover, your pet, your wardrobe
National Enquirer *Star*	the ghost at your start-up facility, the extraterrestial you hired for your first employee, how you lost 175 pounds on a diet of white-out and copy machine powder

Honing Your Start-Up Legend

Whatever media attention you receive, remember to have a colorful version of how your venture started up. Part of the appeal of entrepreneurial literature is its emphasis on the American odyssey from rags to riches. Everyone reading your story will want to believe they can make a million, too. Thus, it behooves you to exaggerate the hardships endured on the way to fame and fortune. Reporters and readers alike will appreciate the good copy a struggling start-up saga makes.

Always characterize the location of your start-up as dingy, damp, cramped, dark, rat-infested, unheated, unsanitary, bombed-out, borrowed, sweltering, depressing, or condemned. Even if you started in beautiful office space, tell interviewers you spent your first few months in a garage, basement, abandoned gas station, old Dairy Queen, unoccupied taco stand, World War II bomb shelter, or still-occupied horse stable. A spare bedroom will get some empathy from readers, but a spare or main bathroom is even better for a start-up locale. Rehearse your story carefully so that you don't give out discrepant details to rival publications. You don't want to become a journalistic cause célèbre just because you told *Venture* that you kept your Kaypro in the bathtub and *Success!* that it sat on the back of the toilet.

Accompany the tale of physical hardship with long accounts of early financial woes. Details can include a completely depleted personal savings account, the sale or remortgaging of your home, your child's forced return to the public school system, and the number of weeks, months, or years you and employees went without regular paychecks. Be sure to emphasize the 14-hour work days and any other pertinent downside information such as divorce or disease. Then sit back and enjoy the rest of your interview by telling outrageous lies about your present personal net worth.

MEGA-LIFESTYLE EVENTS FOR THE VERY ENTRECHIC:

Private audience and venture capital deal with the Pope.
Introduction to Queen Elizabeth and Princess Di.
Invitation to White House and meeting with Mr. T.
Marriage to royal personage or movie star.
Nobel Prize (if William Shockley did it, so can you).
Knighthood (it helps to be British, like Sir Clive Sinclair).
Host for silicon-related disease telethon.
Feature story in the *Esquire Register*.
Opportunity to run Olympics.
Guest appearance on TV sitcom.
Starring role in American Express commercial.
Celebrity judgeship on "Dance Fever."
Cameo role in James Bond movie.
Congressional witness on "Drugs and the Entrepreneur."
Successful race for Senate seat.
Vice Presidential nomination.
Book on best seller list in America and Japan.

The Rewards of Awards

Should your enterprise become worth more than one hundred million, you are likely to become the recipient of several of the numerous awards used by institutions and associations as clever bait for future contributions. Accept all awards, especially ones in which you get to wear a funny hat or a college robe. Your parents will be impressed, and will experience a renewed sense of guilt because they never believed you would amount to anything.

Many entrepreneurs are unaware that they can negotiate the terms of awards in the same way they can any deal. When a university offers you an honorary degree, hold out for an assurance of major press coverage. Tell organizations that an award must be called "Businessman of the Century" or "Entrepreneur of the Eighties" before you'll even think of accepting. Playing hardball with awards committees pays off in better headlines for you and your enterprise.

What to Do A.S.O. (After Selling Out)

The price of spectacular success is often boredom. Once an entrepreneur has seen his or her dream come true, it's time to move on to the next project. Or to get a significant hobby that will make or lose immense amounts of money. If you're about to sell your enterprise, leave a company you took public, or go stir crazy managing an already successful enterprise, you should already be casting about for new risks to take. Here are some of the avocational choices available.

START-UP REDUX

The most obvious answer, of course, is to attempt another start-up. In fact, why not try several? You'll find it easier to raise capital on your new track record, and a lot of anxiety that was there the first time will have dissipated. But beware of the downside of this undertaking. Attempting a new start-up after a successful venture is a little like having another baby when the first one's already in college. You might resent being up in the middle of the night the second time around. So might your spouse. To avoid a feeling of déjà vu, try to pick a slightly different field. Also stop reading entrepreneurial magazines during this period to guard against the dreaded SUAS (Start-Up Addiction Syndrome), in which sufferers feel compelled to begin scores of ventures within a few months of each other.

REAL ESTATE DEALS

Quite a few sold-out types plow mega-capital gains into real estate investments. Buying and reselling land and buildings can get to be quite a fun game, and you could find yourself a budding real estate entrepreneur. It's also a prime way to seek shelter from the tax man (see Gimme Shelter, below).

RESTAURANT MAVENHOOD

It takes a lot of power lunching to cut the kinds of deals you've cut. Your strong feelings about dining atmospheres would make it a cinch to start up a chow palace. Silicon Valley star Nolan Bushnell, late of Atari, opened the very successful Lion and Compass restaurant. Think of a restaurant business as networking insurance.

DROPOUT MOVES

Only for the most desperate or true bleeding-heart liberals, dropout ventures can include nonprofit agencies, relief drives for nonentrepreneurial countries, and marathon walks across the country to redistribute your personal wealth. More lucrative "get away from it all" enterprises include leisure-oriented start-ups such as cruise companies, wine tours of France, or arranged archeological expeditions.

IMPRESARIOSHIP

Running rock festivals or special events such as the Miss Silicon Pageant or Mr. Megabyte Muscle Tournament is a good way to rack up capital losses and make a name for yourself in the press. If you do a good enough job, the powers that be might just make you Baseball Commissioner.

SPORTS TEAM OWNERSHIP

If you always wanted to be a professional athlete, the next best thing means buying a real live sports team. Harold Katz, diet company entrepreneur, owns the Philadelphia 76ers basketball team; McDonald's president Ray Kroc owned the San Diego Padres; and real estate maven Donald Trump owns the USFL New Jersey Generals. Sports teams make a perfect entrepreneurial hobby that provides a lot of media access (coverage in both the business and sports sections) and sometimes even a chance to talk to the President on national television.

Gimme Shelter: The Boredom of Tax Havens

Capital gains are a way of life for the successful entrepreneur. While cashing in stock in your company or selling out for mega-millions, you also must start searching for a way to shelter the lucre. Sheltering immense amounts of money isn't usually a risk-taking activity, and there are only a few things you should know about it:

1. Tax shelters are like wine: there are foreign and domestic types. Learn as little as humanly possible about them, or otherwise you will be tempted to monopolize party conversations with talk of "the best" shelters and their "noses."

2. The truly entrechic never allow their unique drive and ambition to be co-opted in a full-time search for mundane tax shelters. They'd rather be starting up another start-up while the more boring people, their lawyers and accountants, seek protective investments for their millions.

3. Lawyers and accountants will never suggest the really risky, fun ways to lose thousands that will give you lots of losses to report to Uncle Sam. You have to forge ahead and find the dry oil wells or failing world's fairs on your own.

POWER MUNCHING: ENTREPRENEURIAL EATS

All this nonsense specifying that "power lunches" in the business world must consist of heavy meats and "manly" drinks such as martinis does not apply to the entrepreneurial lifestyle. Entrepreneurs represent a New Age type of macho. They like to "graze" rather than eat, a fact that marketing analysts are just waking up to. With no set hours, an entrepreneur will grab a quick bite at any time of day. He or she is an omnivore who worries about roughage while eating Twinkies and dreams about Twinkies while eating raw broccoli. The truly entrechic have a favorite carcinogenic soft drink but also know the difference between mung sprouts and alfalfa sprouts and have no fear of tofu or tempeh.

The entrepreneurial deal-cutting restaurant reflects a California influence, with a smattering of nouvelle cuisine, a bit of ethnic cooking, fresh fruits for the health-conscious and lavish desserts for the sugar and caffeine set. If there is a self-consciousness about what constitutes a "power lunch," it does not focus on the heartiness of the food, but rather its unusual quality. An entrepreneur might not want to admit to another that he hasn't yet tried gladiola flowers filled with salmon mousse.

DEALS AND MEALS

Old Age Power Lunch	New Age Power Munch
Shrimp cocktail	Sashimi
Steak	Veal
Lobster	Bay scallops
Chocolate cake	Ultrachocolate cake
Coffee	Espresso

WINE, THE DRINK OF ENTREPRENEURS

Some people might get the mistaken idea that wine is popular in entrepreneurial circles because of its more generalized appeal to Baby-Boomers aged 25 to 45. Actually, entrepreneurs love California wines because (1) they think of them as entrepreneurial potions bottled in the Land of Mega-Opportunity; and (2) winemakers are themselves entrepreneurs forced to take risks and battle the odds of making millions of dollars.

Becoming a vintner or a winemaker is a very acceptable and entrechic step to take after your first few enterprises yield mega-bucks. A strip of Napa Valley grape land that goes through a couple of bad seasons can make a wonderful tax shelter, too.

SILICON VALLEY OF THE DOLLS: ENTREPRENEUR AS SEX OBJECT

Money has gone from being dirty to being sexy in the space of the last ten years, so it's no surprise that the entrepreneur would also emerge as a sex symbol in the 1980s. The age of the wimp—personified by publicly sensitive types like Alan Alda, William Agee, and Phil Donahue—has given way to worship of the macho venturer. Unfortunately, it is chiefly male entrepreneurs who have benefited from this new sexy status. The entrepreneuse still comes across as too forceful and aggressive to register as a true sex symbol. While we realize that a rotund body type, baldness, or a lack of height could prevent some entrepreneurs from fitting the perfect entresex profile, we list vital characteristics here in the hope that body transplants may be available by the 1990s.

The EntreSex Symbol

Sex: Male
Age: 25–45
Height: 6 feet or over
Weight: 220 or under
Eyes: Intense
Forehead: Slightly wrinkled
Freckles: Optional
Legs and arms: Long
Bodily description: Long, lanky, lean, wiry, slim, athletic
Hair: Long and thick enough to toss back or run fingers through

You can see the entresex symbol out running early in the morning or late at night, tooling around the countryside in his Porsche, or accompanying a movie star to Los Angeles or New York nightspots.

THE FAMILY SCENARIO: IS THERE ACCESS TO NORMALCY?

Entrepreneurs are already married to their enterprises, so much so that those electing to become spouses of lone venturers must accept the pervasive air of bigamy that hangs over their marriages. The prognosis for a healthy marriage in an entrepreneurial setting is not good: the divorce rate among the self-employed and entrechic is high, and so are the therapy bills. Nevertheless, we don't wish to discourage those who spend part of their after-hours time engaged in meaningful relationships. As long as you bear in mind that the enterprise comes first, you can attempt as many marriages as you wish and still make it into the upper echelons of the entrechic pantheon. It just pays to have a lawyer on retainer for personal as well as business purposes.

Below are the various permutations of the entrepreneurial marital structure.

THE START-UP COUPLE

In these relationships any and sometimes all of the following occur, in any order: Boy meets girl, boy and girl get capital, boy and girl get married, boy and girl start up business, boy and girl lose business, boy and girl become enormously successful, boy loses girl, girl loses boy, business loses boy and girl.

THE ENTRECHIC ROMANCE

One spouse is already on his or her way to entrepreneurial success and has a bit of time to relax. He or she marries a nonentrepreneurial type who is either a stable sort like a doctor, lawyer, or accountant, or a chronic underachiever content to listen to every minute detail about "Baby"—XYZ Corporation.

THE ENTREMERGER

A rare occurrence that makes the sparks fly: two entrepreneurial CEOs meet at a seminar or awards ceremony and set up house together. They swap shop stories long distance and set aside an hour of "quality time" each week to sit in the jacuzzi and talk about the week's media interviews.

THE START-UP FAMILY

Mom and Dad were normal employees until the entrepreneurial itch struck. Now the whole family has gotten in on the act. The seven-year-old answers the company phone in the basement and the four-year-old licks stamps and gives interviews to *Weekly Reader* about plans for going public. Meanwhile, Mom breastfeeds baby number three while she assembles microcircuitry boards or trays of canapes.

Dangers of the Start-Up Family

Children tend to regard any environment thrust upon them as normal. While studies show that entrepreneurship runs in families, we can see the difficulties facing young tykes who have no choice but to aspire to entrechicdom at a tender age. Kids who become too intimately involved in a family start-up project have peculiar problems. How exciting can a class trip be when you've flown with Dad to Taiwan to inspect an exporter's disk-drive plant? How can you enjoy the risks inherent in sports such as baseball when you've seen Mom cut deals during her hang gliding lesson? And how can you explain a failing grade in multiplication in third grade when you already know your way around a spreadsheet?

A wise entrepreneurial parent should take time off from a busy schedule to make sure his or her child is not exhibiting any signs of start-up burnout. Children have become too involved in your entrepreneurial goals when:

• They ask for "adventure capital" instead of an allowance.
• They refer to their homework as "R&D."
• They request equity in your company instead of Christmas presents.
• They sign a book contract to write *Entre-Mommy Dearest*.
• They remove the brakes from their bicycles to experience risk-taking firsthand.

ENTREVIEW

**Deirdre Meadows of Mrs.
Meadows' Peanut Butter
and Jelly Sandwiches, Inc.**

       Fad foods and fast foods are now some of America's biggest moneymakers. And right in the thick of this new and lucrative market is Deirdre Meadows. She and her husband, Ron, started Mrs. Meadows' Peanut Butter and Jelly Sandwiches five years ago; today, it is a national franchise worth over $30 million. When Entrechic visited her in her Nevada home, she was busy whipping up a tasty new product: cream cheese and jelly sandwiches.

Entrechic: *It looks like you still take a lot of your work home with you even though Mrs. Meadows' is an astounding success.*
Meadows: Yes, I still brainstorm almost all our new products out of ingredients I have around the house.

EC: *Your customers' familiarity with the ingredients of your products seems to be a key to the success of Mrs. Meadows. How did you come across the idea to provide ordinary, extremely cheap foods at upscale prices?*
Meadows: It all started when I made some peanut butter and jelly sandwiches as appetizers for a potluck dinner Ron and I went to. The guests raved about them. Most loved the authenticity of detail. You see, I never fool around with tradition. I make my basic peanut butter and jelly sandwiches the exact way my mom made them. There's the smooth, pastelike commercial brand of peanut butter and the purple jelly that looks like old Jell-O. And I never put them on any kind of bread but the real "squooshy" white stuff that gets pressed flat in lunch boxes. People just go mad with nostalgia. You have to remember, some of us Baby-Boomers ate peanut butter and jelly sandwiches every day of our childhoods.

EC: *But isn't it true that you do indeed sell variations on the basic sandwich?*
Meadows: Yep. At three ninety-five a pound, our basic PBAJs are our best sellers. But we've discovered that some adventurous types like to see *nouvelle* variations of the old standard. So we do sell PBAJs on black bread and on croissants, and we have a special sandwich made with macadamia nut butter and kiwi jelly. Our dessert PBAJs, made with crushed oreos and M&Ms in the peanut butter, are a real favorite with the after-theater crowd. And everything is made fresh that day at all our stores.

EC: So you might introduce cream cheese and jelly next?

Meadows: Our market research indicates it will do well in certain areas of the country.

EC: What's next after that for Mrs. Meadows'? Will you expand or diversify into new markets?

Meadows: It's a pretty exciting time here, because we're about to run a trial program on a whole new eating concept. It involves another childhood favorite food of many people, canned ravioli and spaghetti. We're buying the cans wholesale from the manufacturers. Then we open and cook each can to order right in front of the customer, who chooses garnishes like a roll and butter, carrot sticks, parsley, or a glass of milk in a Flintstones glass. The customer only has to open the plastic bowl when he or she gets home. We're calling it the "Mama Mia Meadows."

EC: And what will be the retail price?

Meadows: Probably around four ninety-five. After all, we're talking about a complete and nutritious meal that's emotionally satisfying, too.

5

ATTACK OF THE TEENPRENEURS: ENTRECHIC ON CAMPUS

By far the hottest incubators of entrepreneurial talent going today are this nation's colleges and universities. The real reason Johnny can't read is that he's out starting a privately held corporation. Five years ago, every ambitious student wanted an MBA and a promising entry-level job with a large corporation. Now, only losers plan to spend their lives in the corporate treadmill. The new student dream is to go it alone or hook up with a couple of other geniuses to found an enterprise that will make retirement possible at the age of 28. Members of this new breed of aspiring moguls take computer courses on the off chance that their mega-millions concept will fall into the high-tech category. They attend regular business courses so they can check up on their accountants. They even manage to squeeze in a few of the many New Age courses designed to increase the efficiency of teenage entrepreneurs. (Over 250 universities now offer an entrepreneurial curriculum.)

Security-minded parents worry about the new phenomenon. As with many other diseases, entrepreneurial fever hits young people harder than their older counterparts. If the desire to become one of the business world's entrechic types strikes before the age of 19, chances are that fever-induced start-ups will become a chronic, life-long condition that will prove either extremely lucrative or debilitating. Fearful and ignorant of the benefits of the entrechic lifestyle, groups of parents have collaborated with human resources managers of major conglomerates in unsuccessful efforts to quash the collegiate entrepreneurial spirit. Only several months ago, for example, a secret agent from the multibillion-dollar Colossal Profits

Company was apprehended while removing copies of *Inc.* and *Venture* from a campus bookstore. As police removed him from the scene, he cried out, "I'm trying to save these youngsters from eighteen-hour days!"

Surely, such parental and corporate paranoia stem from a total lack of comprehension about the benefits this New Age economy offers college-age entrepreneurs. But you, the grown-up possessor of entrechic, should also be paranoid about the new emphasis on start-up studies in today's college curriculum. Think about it. The legions of teenpreneurs arriving at colleges at the beginning of each school year could make your own life tough in one of several ways.

1. Teenagers have high energy levels and good access to drugs. These plain truths make them formidable rivals in the entrepreneurial marketplace. Any 18-year-old starting up a company is bound to handle the all-nighters better than you can, whether he or she does it naturally or with the aid of speed. When starting up your enterprise, don't forget to check out the possible competition at local colleges.

2. Teenpreneurs make excellent copy. Like kittens or puppies, very young entrepreneurs are simply *cuter* than full-grown types, including you. If your enterprise is in a field filled with teen-run firms, chances are ten to one that the pubescent start-ups will receive better publicity.

3. College entrepreneurs fanatically seek role models and concepts. If you live within 50 miles of a college campus, you're liable to be tapped as a guest lecturer for one of the entrepreneurial courses offered there. Watch out. Entrepreneurial students will act like rock fans and fawn all over you. (When Donald Trump visited the Wharton School, hundreds of kids thrust their resumes into his hands.) Don't let their adulation fool you, and don't tell them about any new concepts. Remember, students are desperate for an entrée into the world of mega-millions, and they will stop at nothing (*especially* business majors.) Many's the entrepreneur whose concept has been stolen by a 20-year-old upstart.

TEENPRENEUR TYPES: WHO STUDIES START-UPS?

On any campus, the following types become attracted to the world of entrepreneurial studies:

Congenital go-getters. Nerdy, asocial junior achievers who usually started more than two businesses when still in high school. Now they're at the top of the entrechic campus hierarchy.

The one-minute majors. Major in 15 different subjects before graduating. The decision to become an entrepreneur doesn't require any special sense of commitment. One-minute majors attend all the guest lectures.

Risk junkies. Undergraduates who used to swallow goldfish, streak naked through the dean's office, or take massive doses of heroin. Now they get their kicks starting up small enterprises.

Trust fundamentalists. Those waiting to come into their trust funds at age 21 or 30. These kids decide to find an honorable start-up with which to pass the time.

ENTREQUOTES

"The books in school are telling me stuff I've already done. It's hard for me to sit down and read a book when I know I can go out there and make some money."

Chris Sadler, entrepreneur, C-average student at Baylor University, Texas.

"I promised my parents I wouldn't start a company while I was in college."

Brad Wexler, president, Wharton Entrepreneurial Center (at the Wharton School), founder of three businesses while under the age of 18.

A TYPICAL ENTRESTUDENT ENTERPRISE: VIDEO VIRGINS

College campuses shelter an astounding array of hot new enterprises run by mini-moguls who still use Clearasil and take their laundry home to Mom. We recently visited one such underaged success story.

When University of Virginia student Dick Robbins first came to campus, he was disappointed at the lack of state-of-the-art video and film facilities. The freshman resolved then and there to make extra money to buy the kind of equipment he needed to become the George Lucas of the 1990s. A personal event provided the spark for what would become a lucrative campus enterprise.

"The first month I was at school, I lost my virginity," says the student entrepreneur. "I knew it was probably happening to a lot of my classmates. And then I started thinking. Sexual initiation is a big event in life. When we pass other milestones, our loved ones record the events in pictures. Birth, first day in school, first communion or bar mitzvah—we have photos of all that stuff. Why couldn't I provide a similar memento of the First Time for my friends and compatriots?"

Out of this simple concept, Video Virgins was born. Advertising with fliers and signs in restrooms, V.V. offers to videotape a student's first sexual experience for only $19.95. Robbins currently employs three other students as part-time workers, and has earned enough to set up a soundstage and editing lab in the basement of his dormitory. He has optioned a screenplay about his adventures, *Video Virgins: The Movie,* and has been approached by franchising consultants about going national with his campus service.

How does he respond to those who express horror at the invasion of privacy involved in the Video Virgins operation? "We are a discreet service. All our cameramen station themselves in closets or outside dormitory windows. When our client requests a clandestine filming, the other half of the couple doesn't even have to know he or she is being taped." For a beginning entrepreneur, Robbins shows a keen grasp of possible legal complications. "So far, we haven't had any problems," confides the college senior, "but I do keep a law student on retainer. Even when the client chickens out or is rebuffed in his or her attempt to consummate the event, we still expect payment. It's in the contract each person signs."

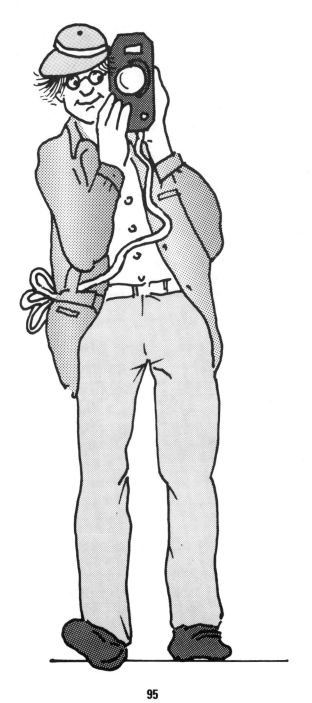

OTHER CHIC COLLEGE ENTERPRISES

"Cliff Notes" Database (user access to all the classics).

Robotic Roommate Service (robot cleans room and fits under bed when members of the opposite sex spend the night).

No Frills Pregnancy Testing (lab business that undersells mass market kits).

Intravenous Caffeine Service (for all-nighters).

Simulated Kidnapping, Inc. (extorts extra spending money from parents through innovative strategies).

Bulimia Barf Bag Service (convenience for those suffering from food disorders).

Downscale Tuition Equity, Inc. (forwards mail and phone calls of students who have moved from Ivy League campuses to state universities without telling their parents. Client and corporation pocket difference in tuition.)

REQUIRED COURSES AT ENTRECHIC U.

The following course descriptions were gleaned from the business school offerings in university catalogs throughout the country.

Entrepreneurial Ego Building. 3 credits. Students will study the works of contemporary egotists, including Muhammed Ali, Hugh Hefner, and Frank Sinatra, as well as classical egotistical material such as the myth of Narcissus. Projects will include the writing of an autobiography and reviews of Barbra Streisand movies. Required text: *People* magazine.

Risk-Taking 101. 3 credits. Students must complete a series of simple exercises, beginning with placing a hand over a lit candle and culminating in a walk through Central Park at midnight with $100 bills pinned to their coats. Video viewing assignments will include films of Karl Wallenda and Evil Knievel.

Advanced Risk-Taking Workshop. 5 credits. Participants will choose among several risk-taking experiences: Dating herpes victims; climbing Mount Everest; ballooning across Siberia; base jumping off the Sears Tower in Chicago. After successfully completing the chosen assignment, students will meet for several "Risky Business" sessions to submit reports of their experiences.

Deal-Cutting Lab. 8 credits. An intensive seminar covering all techniques of deal-cutting, including macho bluster, sheer chutzpah, exaggeration, lying, pleading, begging, and groveling. The second half of the class will be spent in three specially designed lab settings: a ridiculously expensive restaurant, a plush venture capitalist's office, and a bank loan officer's tackily decorated cubicle.

Start-up Lab. 12 credits. Seniors only. A clinic experience in which entrepreneurial interns scout the surrounding community to find the most undesirable start-up facilities. Students whose enterprises go public or whose start-up locations are condemned by the Board of Health automatically receive an extra 4 credits.

Mega-Heroes: The Entrepreneur in Popular Culture. 3 credits. Offered jointly with American Studies Department. Historical readings on important figures in the early Entrepreneurial Movement, including the Wright brothers, Edison, Firestone, and Ford. Comparisons with other pop culture figures such as Superman, Batman, Flash Gordon, and Spiderman. Some emphasis on current affairs and the Entrepreneurial Eighties heroes—Jobs *et al.*

Students Storm President's Office, Demand Venture Capital

DESERT LOOK, CA (EP wire service)–Student protestors from the radical SCS (Students for a Capitalistic Society) today stormed the offices of Death Valley University President Clyde Winters. A spokesperson threatened that the students would occupy the office until the university agreed to set up a venture capital fund for their use. "This school is not looking after our rights as entrepreneurs," said Brett Carp, SCS leader. As he spoke, hundreds of undergraduates chanted, "Fund us, fund us!"

Additional demands include half-price subscriptions to *The Wall Street Journal,* better access to microcomputer software, and an incubator facility in each dormitory building. A spokesperson in the university's public relations office claimed the school already provided a good atmosphere for entrepreneurs. "We have an average of four student-run companies per year going public, along with at least four per year being sold out to larger companies," said the representative. "In addition, the university has gone out of its way to attract entrepreneurial faculty."

The school's most famous faculty member is Abraham Hassenpfeffer, whose 1982 book, *Buy Out This Publisher!,* is widely regarded as an important entrepreneurial manifesto. Hassenpfeffer was away cutting a deal and could not be reached for comment.

THE NEW ENTREPRENEURIAL ASTROLOGY: WHAT'S YOUR ENTRESIGN?

The 1960s and 1970s found the social scene greatly enriched by the appearance of the astrology fad. Instead of asking mundane questions like "Where do you live?" or "What do you do?" partygoers could inquire about astrological signs. Of course, the question "What's your sign?" is now passé, but we believe there should be some similar ice-breaker to ease the social strain of the 1980s. Since everyone is now an entrepreneur, how much easier it would be if we could explain our ambitions through an astrological label.

Here are the new entrescopes, based on the constellations of entrepreneurial "stars," past and present. Consult the chart below to find your own sign according to the date you birthed your first enterprise.

**Edison
(January 1–31)**
You are an inventive sort of person who likes to go to the movies and listen to phonograph records. When you get a good idea, it's like a light bulb goes off in your head. Some time during your life you will invent something that will make you rich and famous. But you are hell to live with.

**Jobs
(February 1–29)**
You are attracted to Eastern mysticism and state-of-the-art gadgets. A short workday for you is 12 hours. You don't trust anyone over 30.

**Marriott
(March 1–31)**
You like to travel and stay in chain hotels. You are not happy unless you can eat a sandwich that's been left in a microwave oven for hours. You watched a lot of Roy Rogers reruns as a kid. You will make tons of money and have your photograph taken a lot.

**Fonda
(July 1–31)**
You enjoy exercise and political causes. Money and guilt come naturally to you. You look great in a bikini.

**Wang
(August 1–31)**
Everybody thinks your company is Japanese, but it's not. (This is very irritating, we know, but don't let it worry you.) You get a kick out of reviving dying industrial towns.

**Famous Amos
(September 1–30)**
You like to balance food on the tips of your fingers. Known for your penchant for hats and casual clothes, you enjoy making guest appearances on television sitcoms.

**Mary Kay
(April 1–30)**
You would never leave the house without wearing makeup. You like the color pink and mink coats. Nobody ever remembers your last name.

**Rubin
(May 1–31)**
You have a tendency to overrationalize every thing you do, and you run with the crowd. Friends and enemies alike are amazed at your chameleonlike temperament, which allows you to surface with a new persona every few years.

**Trump
(June 1–30)**
You like heights and shiny surfaces. As a kid, you played a lot of Monopoly and always ended up owning all the hotels on Boardwalk.

**DeLorean
(October 1–31)**
You like Irish folk music and fast cars. You might be tempted to finance your venture creatively, but don't. Stay away from fashion models and government agents.

**Kroc
(November 1–30)**
Give yourself a lot of breaks—you deserve it. Some of your best friends are clowns. Late in life you might be tempted to buy a baseball team.

**Perdue
(December 1–31)**
You are a brave entrepreneur who never chickens out. Some time in late middle age, you will be discovered as a sex symbol and become the George Burns of television commercials. With an appreciative public egging you on, you'll become a household name.

ENTREVIEW

Joe Smith, Joe Jones, and
Joe Brown, inventors of
Futile Pursuit, a nationally
acclaimed board game

Last Christmas, young professionals went wild over a new board game invented by three young Canadians. Bucking a trend toward video entertainment, the three hit upon a game in which there are no answers for the myriad of questions contained on the playing cards. The Buddha-shaped board encourages meditation and conversation among players.

Our EntreChic reporter talked to all three "good Joes" over espresso and a game of Futile Pursuit.

Entrechic: Given the competitive spirit nowadays, what made you hit upon the idea of such a laid-back game, one with no answers?
Joe Smith: See, that's just it. The eighties *are* ridiculously dog-eat-dog. And our game just isn't, you know? I mean, it's like those late-night bull sessions in the dormitory used to be.
Joe Jones: Yeah. The three of us were sitting around talking one evening after supper and we sort of slipped into that sixties nostalgia stuff. Like, we started saying, "What is the meaning of life?"
Joe Brown: That first night, I remember we brainstormed a whole bunch of questions. You know, stuff like, "How long is infinity?" "Is there life after death?" "How does a swallow know to come back to Capistrano?"
Joe J: From there, the concept just grew. We started writing down the questions on cards. Pretty soon, we even put them on a computer. We had access to all sorts of people—the mailman, our barber, the owner of a local restaurant. We asked them all about the unanswerable questions of their lives.

EC: Did you ever expect Futile Pursuit to be such a hit?
Joe S: Not at all, especially when we first started out. But when I think about it, it makes a lot of sense. I mean, people have to produce answers to questions all day long at their jobs. When they get home at night or go out to friends' houses on the weekends, it must be comforting to think about the intangibles of life.

EC: But even though the idea has been a huge success, it must have been difficult to get financial backing at first.
Joe B: Yeah. I was in charge of that end of it, and I can tell you, it wasn't easy. I knew we needed distribution from a big company, but at first I didn't know how to go about it. I mean, all the other game inventors could show big companies nifty video packages where

little monsters get blown up. All I had was a bunch of cards. Some start-up!

EC: What was your big break?
Joe S: We're ashamed to admit this, but we lied just a bit. We got all the people who had contributed questions to call up game and toy stores and ask when that exciting new game, Futile Pursuit, was going to be available.
Joe J: Altogether, our friends made over two million calls.

EC: Two million?
Joe B: That's what finally did it. The game retailers of America were driving the distributors crazy with requests. So finally, we cut a deal with one of them. And the rest, as they say, is history. (*The two other Joes laugh.*)

EC: We understand that there are more versions of Futile Pursuit in the works. Can you explain how you can compile thousands of unanswerable questions on movie trivia?
Joe S: Oh, our Movie Screen edition was easy. One of the questions was "How come an actress' mascara never runs when she cries?" Another one was "Does Superman ever go to the bathroom?"

EC: We should tell our readers that while we've been talking, we've also been playing the basic Genius edition of Futile Pursuit.
Joe J: Yeah, that's the beauty of it. You can choose how long you and your guests want to ponder a particular rhetorical or unanswerable question. For more than sixty minutes, we've been thinking on "How much wood would a woodchuck chuck if a woodchuck could chuck wood?" That's from our Natural Science category.

EC: Yes, it's certainly been an enjoyable meditation. It's almost a shame to break the spell and bring up the rather unpleasant business of that lawsuit. Isn't it true that you three have been sued by the estate of Jean-Paul Sartre?

Joe S: Damn right. We can't figure it out. They're saying we stole the whole existential concept from him, but it's just not true. As I told you before, it's more like three good buddies shooting the bull.

EC: Well, best of luck with the trial. And good luck with all those ancillary products you launched this year. We especially like the tote bag that has no bottom.

6

INTRAPRENEURS: PRACTICING ENTRECHIC WITHIN CORPORATE WALLS

Most entrepreneurs prefer to start up enterprises of their own, but as entrepreneurial fever envelops every sector of our society, large institutions are beginning to claim that they, too, can foster and fulfill the innovative venturer. According to entrechic consultants, even boring employees in huge corporations can use entrepreneurial prowess to develop and market new products and services. One such expert, Gifford Pinchot III, has dubbed this internal function "intracorporate entrepreneurship," or "intrapreneurship" for short.

The truly entrechic should approach the concept of intrapreneurship with caution. After all, doesn't true entrepreneuring require an element of extreme risk? To those who have put their personal assets and good name on the line, intrapreneuring in a corporate setting seems a little like going mountain climbing on an asphalt driveway or scuba diving in a four-foot-deep swimming pool.

Still, if you are not quite ready to make the break from the established, old-line business world, intrapreneurship just might provide a transitional step into the world of entrechic. Becoming a venturer within corporate walls can help you sample some of what entrepreneurship has to offer without forcing you to forego the regular paycheck that spouses, mortgage companies, and orthodontists come to expect over the years.

BOSS-BUSTERS: A STARTLING NEW CONCEPT

After years of thinking that bigger is better, American companies now extoll the innovative benefits of decentralization. Scrambling to disassociate themselves from bigness, corporations have begun to ridicule and reject a formerly cherished resource: the company man. Move over, Man in the Gray Flannel Suit. It's time to make way for the Idea Champion. An idea champion acts brashly, takes risks, cuts through all kinds of red tape, and moves as a free agent through the once-rigid corporate bureaucracy. This ingenious boss-buster will someday invent a product that will revolutionize the industry, and a large corporation wants to make sure that the product comes out under its rubric and not under the logo of a start-up company that the idea man has founded on his own.

To attract and foster boss-busters, a large firm must try very hard to change its "culture," or inner workings. The old bureaucratic, hierarchichal structure doesn't work for innovative ideas. The most excellent ideas, say the business experts, come out of entrepreneurial companies. This means that if you're entrepreneurially inclined, big corporations will beat a path to your door. And, if you're currently stuck in a dead-end corporate job, you might be able to get ahead with a little intrapreneurial verve. The barriers to corporate success are tumbling down for the average employee who can take a suggestion he would normally mumble under his breath and offer it to the CEO.

How does all this idea championing affect the normal course of promotions and steps up the corporate ladder? We've followed the career of one up-and-coming intrapreneur, Lenny Q, as he innovated his way to personal and financial success.

INTRAPRENEUR EXTRAORDINAIRE: THE CASE OF LENNY Q

Lenny Q first worked for Superior Slingshot and Nuclear Armaments Co. during his summer vacations from college in 1968 and 1969. He was then in charge of cleaning the lunchroom. While emptying the trash one day in July, 1969, Lenny began wondering about the possible usefulness of discarded yogurt container lids. After collecting them for several days, he took the pile into the company machine shop, where, using the lids as wire holders, he brainstormed a new soldering technique that later saved the company $5 million dollars a year in production costs. The suggestion was enough to get him noticed by company officers, who offered him a job cleaning the machine shop after he graduated from college.

Of course, the company brass had no idea that isolating Lenny from lunch debris, his original source of stimulation, was the worst thing it could do to encourage innovation. But despite these obstacles, Lenny went on to perform like a true intrapreneur. In his first three years on the job, he was able to discover a new polymer resin after accidentally melting his broom handle over a Bunsen burner, and a superior adhesive material made from metal shavings and human saliva. Unfortunately, some of his channels to the top levels of the company had closed up during those years, and only the polymer resin reached the open market. But Lenny had other irons in the fire, too. He sometimes went over to the lunchroom after closing hours to bootleg raw materials for experimentation. On one such occasion, he fashioned a child's doll out of plastic drinking straws that later netted over $450 million for the company's toy division.

Lenny's intrapreneurial successes brought him new power within the company. The president directed the accounting department to give the innovator $1000 to use on any company project. And soon, Lenny was promoted to head janitorial facilitator, with responsibility for all the restrooms as well as the machine shop and lunchroom. He used his directed capital to establish a for-profit day care center in the ladies' rooms on the first and third floors of the corporate facility, plus a fast-food enterprise, Lenny's Latkes, in a corner of the lunchroom.

In 1977, Superior Slingshot sold the Lenny's Latkes Franchise division of the company to General Foods for over $410 million. This divestiture freed some of Lenny's time, and he took a three-week sabbatical to write *Brainstorming with a Broom,* his seminal work on intrapreneurship that has been on *The New York Times* best seller list for over eight years. While appearing on one of the many television talk shows for his book publicity tour, Lenny fixed a faulty video camera by inventing a revolutionary new lens. The new camera, manufactured by Superior Slingshot and Nuclear Armaments, later became standard equipment for NASA space shuttle flights.

But Lenny is not one to rest on his intrapreneurial laurels. Today he is vice president for janitorial services, and has a staff of three reporting to him and helping him brainstorm new ideas. His restless intrapreneurial personality has led him to invent a new microcomputer with a screen made of a used hub cap, a high-protein food substance extracted from cardboard that might someday feed the Third World, and an ergonomically designed, self-cleaning mop. Gone are the days when he had trouble gaining access to the company's top echelons. High-level executives regularly come to the basement to swap jokes and learn about new ideas. Sometimes they even take up the broom beside him as he goes on regular inspection rounds. And Elmer Lund, current president of the company, has established the Lenny Q Internship, which provides lunchroom janitorial positions for bright young men and women just out of college.

When reporters or other nosy folks suggest that Lenny could have made millions of dollars in the outside world as an entrepreneur, he demurs. "I suppose so, but this is a regular living, with nice people. I always had health insurance coverage, you know. This company's been good to me. I have a lot of autonomy. Why would I have wanted to leave?"

AN INTRAPRENEURIAL GUIDE TO CORPORATE CULTURES

To understand the sudden flowering of intrapreneurial talent in the 1980s, we must go back to the corporate cultures of the previous decades. Here is a brief history of the recent development of working atmospheres in America.

1949–1966: Yeast Culture. The smokestack industrial economy continued to grow. Lots of oil meant lots of cars, lots of steel, and lots of workers. Profits rose like bread overnight. Companies with hierarchical structures flourished.

1967–1975: Counter Culture. During this antibusiness era, the vibes weren't good in either entrepreneurial or intrapreneurial circles. Meanwhile, oil prices went through the roof and the economy began to deteriorate. The seeds of the Information Revolution were sown, but conglomerates continued to be staffed by short-haired people who had "bosses."

1976–present: Yogurt Culture. The hand of fate reached to the bottom of the business world's yogurt carton and mixed in the fruits and nuts with the blander substance. Business is now sexy, funny, exciting, nonhierarchical. It's not cool to have a boss or be a boss. Even if a person works for a big company, it's just a division or small unit. Idea champions reign supreme.

PATHWAYS TO INTRAPRENEURSHIP

As established companies find themselves competing in the marketplace with start-up ventures, they are developing human resources strategies to hire and retain intrapreneurial types. Large corporations now try one or several of the following approaches to develop an intrapreneurial culture for their employees.

HIRE THE MALADJUSTED

One of the best ways to stir up a company and bring in a new culture is to hire alienated, independent types who won't get along with anyone else. If you have always been the kind of thorn-in-the-side person who annoys everyone around you, this intrapreneurial hiring period could be your window to career opportunities. We eavesdrop here on a snippet of a typical recruiting interview with a company desperate to foster intrapreneurship.

Company: Hello. Nice to meet you.
Intrapreneur: What a mundane thing to say.
Company: Oh really? How interesting. What would *you* say at the beginning of an interview?
Intrapreneur: To begin with, I wouldn't even hold stupid interviews. I think running a triathlon would be a better test of risk-taking and endurance.
Company: Oh. Well, let's move on to our next question. How do you see yourself in five years?
Intrapreneur: Christ, that old chestnut! Speaking honestly, I would expect to be out of this dump by then. Of course, I'll have invented at least five products, setting new standards in the industry. Naturally, you guys will make all the bucks off them, which might really tick me off. So I'd have to get out and start up my own company to beat the pants off of you. I'd just be marking time here, but it would be worth your while. I think I could straighten out all the screwups in the first six months and then be free to start innovating. Of course, I would expect an autonomous budget and complete control over every facet of my operation.
Company: Of course. When would you start?
Intrapreneur: As soon as you fire that clown of a president.

ACQUIRE A START-UP VENTURE

If you can't breed innovation, buy it. That's the motto of huge corporations that acquire entrepreneurial enterprises and make them a small part of their large happy family. Corporations buy not only the product and ideas of companies, but in some cases, the entrepreneur who started up the whole she-bang.

If you're a micro-enterprise owner wearying of the entrepreneurial world, getting co-opted into the land of conglomerates isn't a bad deal. In most cases, you're offered stock in the parent company and a hefty salary or consulting fee. An entrepreneur turned intrapreneur still stands at the helm of a "division," enjoying the best of both worlds: cutting-edge leadership opportunities *and* a pension plan. Plus, your parents will be proud that "your" company sponsors the Olympics.

CAPITALIZE ON ACCIDENTS

Also called the "penicillin approach," this strategy relies on employees at all levels tinkering with products and services. Company literature extolls heroes who brought startling innovations to the attention of their superiors. No one writes about all the employees who get fired because they're fooling with stuff while their other work goes undone.

START START-UPS AND SKUNKWORKS

By far the most popular approach to creating an intrapreneurial culture is the establishment of entrepreneurial ghettos in certain areas of a large corporation. In some cases, corporate management hand-picks a group of men and women to leave the fold and start up a new enterprise and then take it public, with a substantial share of equity remaining with the parent company. Or, in another type of situation, the large corporation simulates start-up conditions in the outside world for a small department of workers involved in a special project. (One such simulated start-up facility came complete with a leaky roof to inspire triumph over hardship.) Related to intrapreneurial start-ups are skunkworks, whole divisions or depart-ments where nerdy weirdos slug away at seemingly meaningless product innovations that sometimes yield spectacular results. These skunks receive a limited budget and very little corporate attention. Once they come up with something marketable, it's usually stolen by a more charismatic idea champion, and the skunks go back to their smelly nests to root around for new concepts.

Skunks, so dubbed because of their undesirability as corporate executives, are very low on the intrapreneurial totem pole, and hence on the entrechic status scale. They're the corporate equiva-lent of the guys and gals who ran the audiovisual equipment in high school. They love gadgets but have trouble communicating with other people. If you aspire to intrapreneurship, get to know a skunk, but don't become one yourself.

INTRACAPITAL: MANAGING YOUR COMPANY'S MONEY

One key to intrapreneurial success is obtaining "intracapital," sums of money given to employees to be used at their discretion. The amount can vary anywhere from $5 (coffee and donuts for the office) to $100,000 (a new donut-machine design). Some companies have formal intrapreneurial programs in which employees apply for funds to start up intraprises. Others simply wait for self-starters to come forward and demand intracapitalization. Your best approach for requesting such funds will, of course, depend on your networking ties in the corporation and on the culture of the company involved.

Here are samples of official documents pertaining to the re-quest for intracapital.

The Bureaucratic Company

Application for Intracapital, Widgetronics, Inc.

NAME: Preston Chipley

JOB TITLE: Assistant to the Assistant Vice President in Charge of Assistant Vice Presidents

YEARS WITH COMPANY: 21

AMOUNT REQUESTED: $5,000

SUGGESTED INTRAPRISE: A new "rat" device for operating microcomputers. Bigger and better than the standard "mouse," the Widgerat will enable four people at once to perform on-screen functions. Instead of a conference call, the rat will facilitate a conference input.

In Two Paragraphs, Let Your Boss Tell Why You Out Of All Widgetronics Employees Should Receive An Intracapital Grant.

It was a great pleasure when Mr. Chipley came to me with a vague idea about building a better mouse. Once he and I had brainstormed for hours and I had provided the necessary direction he needed to properly verbalize his concept, I encouraged him to think about applying for this grant. I assure you that Mr. Chipley is a very hard worker who will not spend any of the company's precious time fooling around with this frivolous notion. However, should he get it to amount to something by working after hours and weekends, I also feel confident that he will turn over all findings for the good of the common corporate weal.

In conclusion, I would like to add in all sincerity that it is rare when a drone like Mr. Chipley actually comes up with something interesting. But with my intrapreneurial guidance and example, he just might come through.

Reginald Modester

Reginald Modester
Assistant Vice President in Charge of Assistant Vice Presidents

The Semi-Intrapreneurial Company

WIDGETRONICS

September 15, 1985

Mr. Tom Braverman
Director
IntraCapital Program
Widgetronics, Inc.
Denver, Colorado

Dear Tom:

    I am writing to request a $5,000 grant from the IntraCapital Program. After more than two decades with Widgetronics, I think I know a lot about how a new concept becomes market-ready, and I would like the opportunity to develop a new product. I have already built a prototype of the Widgerat, a new light-sensor device similar to a "mouse." I estimate that the total project would eventually require more than $5000, but that amount would give me and my staff the ability to build several more prototypes and do some marketing surveys.

    Please let me know if you would like more information about my concept or my performance record here at the company. And say hello to Madge and the kids.

Sincerely,

Pres Chipley
Pres Chipley
Associate Director of
Hierarchies

The Totally Intrapreneurial Company

From the Desk of Pres Chipley

Tom, baby—
listen, I need 5
thou for this wild
concept we're kicking
around down here. I'll
tell you about it at
tennis—hope you can
swing the dough, 'cause
I think it's _real hot!_

Pres

Intrapreneurship at a Glance

Advantages	Disadvantages
Free business cards	Fair degree of anonymity
Insurance benefits	Absence of juicy tax deductions
Camaraderie	Daily contact with inferior minds
Steady income	No mega-millions
Access to internal venture capital	Accountability to bureaucrats

---

The Ultimate in IntraChic:
"Wasteland Start-Up" Operated by International Big Business Machines

(Last June, our Entrechic reporter investigated firsthand one of the many intrapreneurial start-up centers springing up across the country. Here is his report.)

"This kind of start-up management is really the wave of the future for large corporations," said Henry Basehart, director of the IBBM Start-up Skunkworks, as he pushed a button to call up the elevator from underground. Basehart's pinstriped countenance stood out against the stark landscape as we waited for the elevator to ascend. Located in the eroded Badlands of South Dakota, the facility simulates some of roughest conditions under which an entrepreneur could work.

"The idea was to challenge some of our most intrapreneurial employees with mega-tough start-up conditions and see if they could come up with truly innovative products," added the manager as we descended into the facility. We were already familiar with other elements of the IBBM Simu-Start-Ups across the nation. At one, the company sprinkled cans of live cockroaches into the basement facility; at another frigid Midwestern location, start-up types did without a furnace for an entire winter season. "Just because we're corporate doesn't mean we're cushy," has become a well-known IBBM slogan. But nothing we had heard about the other IBBM start-ups prepared us for our first glimpse of the Badlands facility.

117

More than 80 feet underground, the Wasteland unit houses 12 intrapreneurs ranging in ages from 17 to 39, eight males and four females. After stepping off the elevator, we began to walk up a glassed-in ramp that looked out on about 1000 square feet of total squalor. Basehart quickly noted that the start-up subjects could not see us behind the one-way mirror. Huddled in three small groups, the intrapreneurs were half-naked and unwashed. One woman was cooking what looked like a small dog carcass over an open fire. A man in the corner was working on a transistor radio. Another was scratching what seemed to be a poem into the dirt floor with a sharp stick.

"I can see the look of shock on your face," said Basehart, smiling. "No matter how hard we try to prepare observers for this facility, it's impossible to cushion the impact of seeing it for the first time. This is the ultimate start-up. Whereas our other operations merely introduce the element of hardship into a modern setting, this facility simulates conditions after a nuclear holocaust."

But what can a modern corporation possibly gain from enforcing such start-up conditions? A lot, according to Basehart. "By removing the normal distractions and fancy crutches people use as excuses for complacency in their daily lives, this start-up facility helps intrapreneurs focus on basic products that could lead to a whole way of rethinking technology in the future. We don't expect particular projects to emerge for at least a decade, but the *process* by which these 'post-holocaust' intrapreneurs organize a new company will provide us with information we can use to structure a more effective corporate unit."

Ten years? We asked the Simu-Start-Up manager how many times intrapreneurs would rotate through the Badlands facility during that period. "Only once. We feel that to be most effective, the same group must work together under these adverse conditions for as long as possible. But don't worry. All these people are sufficiently compensated for their time and effort. Since they don't need conventional money sources while in the start-up shelter, all their salary and bonuses are earning high interest in special accounts. Just think how wonderful it will be to have survived the ultimate in start-up hardships and then come out to a tidy nest egg!"

CULTURE SHOCK: NEW WAVE INTRAPRENEUR VS. OLD WAVE PINSTRIPE

Unfortunately, not all companies or all employees react well to the new concept of intrapreneurship. As a budding intracorporate entrepreneur, you might find yourself in an awkward position in the corporate world. Old-line business types don't take kindly to young whippersnappers who want to communicate directly with the higher echelons of the company. And, not surprisingly, most old-wave bosses don't favor "touchy-feely," boss-busting atmospheres. They'll want your climb up the corporate ladder to be just like theirs: slow and dirty.

So how's a guy or gal in search of excellence supposed to work within the system? Before you decide to broach the subject of intrapreneurship with your current boss, consult the following checklist.

Checklist: Is Your Boss Ready for an Intrapreneurial You?

On company business, your boss introduces you to others as "my lackey."
True _____ False _____
When you mention an idea, your boss laughs.
True _____ False _____
Afterward, your boss passes off your idea as his or her own.
True _____ False _____
Your boss practices MBSAY (Management by Standing Around Yelling).
True _____ False _____
You boss thinks *In Search of Excellence* was a late-night television talent show.
True _____ False _____

If you were able to admit that one or more of the above statements are true, your immediate superior represents an impossible barrier to your career as an intrapreneur. If you persist in trying to innovate and develop intraprises, you eventually will be forced to quit and join the mainstream world of entrechic, or you will find yourself fired, thereby becoming an outrepreneur.

THE OUTREPRENEUR: HOW TO REACT CREATIVELY TO A PINK SLIP

For almost all entrepreneurial types trying to carve out a niche within the corporate structure, there comes a day of reckoning when they go past the acceptable limit of risk-taking and receive an invitation to leave the company. In fact, this form of leave-taking has become an accepted rite of passage in entrepreneurial circles. Great men and women feel no shame at being sacked by stodgy corporations. Becoming a temporary outrepreneur can only add to your aura of entrechic. (In interviews about your start-up enterprise, it helps to be able to describe the companies you once worked for as "hopeless dinosaurs.")

Should you finally get the boot after much intrapreneurial exertion, take time to revel in the experience. Feign surprise and make it as difficult as possible for your boss to dismiss your services. If you are fortunate enough to get wind in advance that the axe is about to fall, enlist the aid of friends and loved ones to perform one or several of the following devious acts a couple of days before you go:

1. Get a male friend with an authoritative voice to call constantly, leaving vague messages about a check for $100 million in venture capital funds that he's waiting for you to pick up.

2. Hire someone who looks like Diane Sawyer to come into the office with television cameras and interview you about your latest intrapreneurial product achievement.

3. Take out a full-page ad in your local newspaper thanking the company for the autonomy it has given you and enumerating your triumphs over the months or years you have worked there. Try to find a picture of you and your boss embracing to illustrate the text. End the ad by saying how much you're looking forward to working at XYZ Corp. in the future.

On the actual day when you know you're going to be fired, go into your boss' office smiling and humming, carrying a copy of *Venture* magazine. A typical intrapreneurial dismissal scene might go like this:

Boss: Hi, Hank. Please sit down. A cup of coffee?
You: No, thanks. Hey, Ed, did I ever tell you how much I really appreciate all the support you've given my concepts since I started working here?
Boss: Umm. Oh. Well, I was happy to do it. In the past, you did have some awful good ideas. I know the company appreciated your input.
You: Yeah, well, I sure think this is a swell place. I keep telling all my friends how lucky I am to have such a perfect match for my entrepreneurial skills. I think working here has meant more to me than anything else in my life.
Boss: I didn't realize you had such an affection for the place, especially considering the lack of support for your recent project.
You: A minor disagreement, that's all.
Boss: Hank, I'd hardly call your unauthorized use of ten million bucks to develop "Fe-Lean Cuisine" frozen diet cat food a "minor disagreement." The board of directors held a special meeting about the incident last night.
You: Well, I'm sure after they saw the demographic data, the market survey results, and the veterinarians' testimonials, they decided to go ahead with it. I

admit that bootlegging those funds was a little rash, but sometimes the best products surface through circuitous routes. I'm willing to admit that I'm unorthodox but, in this case, I'm right on the mark. We'd have a ninety-nine percent market share in the space of a few months!

Boss: Sure. Even with a retail price of three forty-nine a package? Look, Hank, I don't know how to tell you this, but there's no "we" anymore. I've received orders to let you go. I'm sorry. Naturally, we can provide some severance pay.

You: Severance pay, hell! What do you think I am, some sissy? I'll tell you what I demand. I demand my cat food concept. It'll fly with a true innovator behind it. Just give me "Fe-Lean Cuisine," or you'll be hearing from my lawyer. [Storm out, making lots of noise. Pause outside door to yell to secretary within earshot of boss.] Get me that venture capital consultant on the phone!

SOME THINGS TO DO THE FIRST DAY YOU BECOME AN OUTREPRENEUR

Issue a press release about your plans for a new venture.
Have business cards made up with your new company logo.
Clean out your garage or basement to use as start-up space.
Start losing weight for next year's *Time* magazine cover photo.

ENTREVIEW

Roland Bushelbasket of Progeny Robotics, Inc.

In the early 1970s, Roland Bushelbasket emerged as one of the brightest of the rising high-tech stars. The enormous success of his fast-paced video game, Fang Fong, enabled him and a few partners to launch a lucrative computer enterprise, Atonassis. After Bushelbasket sold his share in the firm, he went on to found Tortilla Time, a restaurant chain featuring giant automated enchiladas who sang and danced. Unfortunately, the restaurant venture proved less successful and eventually went bankrupt. But Bushelbasket is a man whose engine is constantly on "start-up." Deeply engaged in the initial phases of his new venture, Progeny Robotics, the 44-year-old entrepreneur took time out to talk to our Entrechic reporter.

Entrechic: *Do you ever let the failure of your last venture, Tortilla Time Restaurants, get you down?*
Bushelbasket: Absolutely not! It was real fun, and now that party's over. You really can't dwell on mistakes or you lose your nerve. Like my friend Barney—I'm sorry, I can't tell you his last name—who lost a couple of million last month. He's just been moping around the house driving his wife crazy. What's the big deal? After all, you can't take it with you!

EC: *In the past, you've proven yourself a pretty savvy entrepreneur. To what do you attribute the failure of your restaurant chain?*
Bushelbasket: There were a few factors involved there. For one thing, I totally misread some of the market research. It indicated that Mexican food was on the upswing, and so I just assumed that the public would accept anthropomorphized enchiladas. Since then, I've realized that we should have gone with talking knishes or singing spaghetti. There's an anti-Hispanic bias in this country that's pretty frightening. It seems that people will *eat* an enchilada, but they don't want to be entertained by one that's eight feet tall and sings. I'm appalled by what it says about our cultural climate, but there was nothing I could do to make customers come in if they didn't want to.

EC: *I guess the expertise you and your engineers developed at Tortilla Time hasn't gone totally to waste. I understand your new venture, Progeny Robotics, also hinges on people's acceptance of automation.*
Bushelbasket: Yes, and we're right on the mark this time, if I do say so myself. You see, at Progeny we're designing robot versions of children for busy couples. Essentially, we're in the business of giving people lifestyle choices for the eighties.

EC: *That sounds like an interesting concept. Can you explain your product a little better?*

Bushelbasket: Certainly. We have two basic models, the Nicole 101 and the Zachary 120. Both come with modular add-ons to simulate physical growth, and reprogrammable circuitry to allow mental and emotional development. Infertile couples or couples who just don't want to be bothered with all the childbirth classes and the breathing stuff can pick up a Nicky or Zack at any local toy store. It's initially a portable unit that can wake you up a couple of times a night if you want it to. Later, the unit moves around the house and walks to school itself.

EC: I don't want to appear rude, but we're in the midst of an echo baby boom these days. Why would anyone want to buy an expensive robot when they can make their own child or adopt? And wouldn't a machine version of a child be much less fulfilling to the parent?

Bushelbasket: No on both counts. First of all, our basic models retail for about fifty-one thousand dollars. Now, that might seem like a lot. But when you figure that the average couple spends over two *hundred* thousand raising a child to the age of eighteen, a Progeny purchase represents significant savings. And, to answer your second question, I don't think you can really make generalized statements about parental fulfillment. Psychologists have shown that a lot of parents resent the enormous drain on their time that children represent. Hell, even Dear Abby readers said that if they had it to do over again, seventy-five percent would never have had kids.

A Progeny robo-kid can keep you from making a mistake you'll regret for the rest of your life. And it costs about the same as a Mercedes! If you want to go on vacation, you can just shut down little Zack's system. If you've feeling flush one year, send Nicole to private school. But if your business fails or something, you can withdraw her entirely and leave her in a closet until you can afford a good school wardrobe again. You really spend as much as you want to. If you don't like the idea of day care, for example, the kid doesn't have to go. It'll sit at the kitchen table all day coloring and never move, if you want it to.

And, you know, anyone can get one. Say you want to adopt a live kid. Sometimes you can't if you've ever been divorced or if you're single or gay. With a robo-kid, no one asks any nosy questions.

EC: This is impressive, but there's bound to be a lot of criticism of these "Stepford Kids." Don't you think a lot of social critics will say it represents the ultimate in control, a nightmarish Brave New World, for everyone to have a robotic child?
Bushelbasket: People are stupid that way. That's an old-line way to look at technology. We're talking high-touch technology that fits into lifestyles, *not* something that hinders personal development. Nicky and Zack possess the latest in artificial intelligence technology. Until you've had them more than ten years, you won't notice much difference between their interactive capabilities and those of the flesh-and-blood type kids. You can program them for tantrums and bed-wetting and prolonged cold viruses—all the downside stuff, if you're a true masochist. But you can also choose our Little Angel software and experience only the upside of parenthood. We haven't perfected our Teen Rebel program yet, but when we do, you can choose to skip it or you can have your robo-kid get the whole awkward adolescent trip over with in just a week.

EC: It's absolutely overwhelming. When can we expect to see this product at our local stores?
Bushelbasket: Well, right now we're waiting on some more venture capital to give us the funds we need for marketing. But I'm convinced that by 1990, there'll be a robo-kid on every block.

EC: *It's rude to point this out, we know, but there's a bug in your hair, Mr. Bushelbasket.*

Bushelbasket: No there isn't! This really is an exclusive interview I've granted you here, because I now want to introduce something that's still in the R and D stage: It's De-bug, our Micro-Robot. Gosh, I hope some venture capitalists are reading this. Watch and I'll have the little critter land in your hair, too.

EC: *Thanks, but no thanks.*

7

THE LAZARUS SYNDROME: ENTREPRENEUR REDUX

The average entrepreneur fails 3.8 times before finding the venture that yields mega-millions. So if your first stab at entrechic turns into Chapter 11 of a planned success story, take heart. Just remember that seekers of entrepreneurial fame and fortune never set much stock in spectacular or sputtering types of failure. They rarely ever speak of going under, except to magazine interviewers writing about the mega-implications of their later triumphs. (A good failure story makes just as superlative copy as a start-up hardship saga.) Sure, losing a couple of million bucks hurts, but it does not deter a true entrepreneur from getting back in the start-up saddle again. Entrepreneurial egos are too strong to be bothered by petty details like the repossession of BMWs and hot tubs.

This hardy resilience has a physiological as well as psychological basis in fact. Researchers have found that the bodies of the most successful entrepreneurs harbor a disease known as Lazarus Syndrome. The peculiar affliction allows those whose business careers are presumed dead and rotting to suddenly spring up, full of new start-up and go. Blood samples taken from a random number of entrepreneurs indicate a "comeback" microbe that was also found in the blood of Richard Nixon, Adam Osborne, and Sir Freddie Laker. Early signs of the Lazarus Syndrome include a nauseatingly high level of optimism in the face of disaster and a pathological desire to lie about one's financial assets.

From historical documents, we can estimate that a small percentage of the population has always harbored the Lazarus microbe. These are the folks who repeatedly rebuilt burnt-out cities, used their last funds to sail for America on crowded cargo ships, and sang as the *Titanic* went down.

Without actually taking the blood test (which, owing to its mega-price, is not yet available in a home kit version), it is difficult to determine if you suffer from Lazarus Syndrome. One way to tell, of course, is if you've ever lost more than $3 million dollars and then recouped it in less than a year. However, if you are not yet in the midst of your alloted 3.8 failures, we have found another way to determine if you have been exposed to the Lazarus microbe. First, read the following credo.

The Credo of the Entrepreneur Redux

I believe Liz Taylor will be happy with her next husband.

I believe prime-time television programming will improve in the coming years.

I believe the next President of the United States will be a Catholic woman or a Black Muslim.

I believe that everyone will someday learn how to pronounce the new versions of Chinese city names.

Do these statements sound plausible to you? If the answer is yes, you've already been bitten by the bug that will endow you with tremendous flexibility and stamina in the entrepreneurial marketplace. For those who crave all that entrechic offers, the Lazarus Syndrome is indeed a fortunate disease.

LAZARUS ROLE MODELS: STARTING OVER

Is fear of failure keeping you from the upper echelons of entre-chic? Here are some stirring examples of heroes who have embraced failure, wrestled it to the ground, and gone on their merry ways.

Sam Honkel, Former President, Disposable Down Products

Eight months after procuring over $4 million in venture capital for his start-up company, Disposable Down Products, President Sam Honkel was selling off inventory and planning to fold the operation. What went wrong?

"We found that the public wasn't ready for disposable goose down vests and coats made of paper," laments the 32-year-old Seattle entrepreneur. "The thirty-nine ninety-five price tag was just too high for one-time wear, even though we were aiming at an affluent market with lots of disposable income. Then, on top of our other problems, the popularity of down clothing plummeted at the beginning of 1985."

Honkel might be down, but not out. Recently he remortgaged his house to get capital for his new operation, Paperback-Pack, a disposable backpack made for day hikers. He foresees sales in the six-figure range by 1987.

Fred Plotzer, Former CEO, ErgoToilet Inc.

Fred Plotzer and two partners invested over $200,000 to start up ErgoToilet, a company to manufacture ergonomically-designed toilets and other bathroom accessories. Now that the company is in bankruptcy proceedings, Plotzer concedes that the product was before its time. "I think it's ridiculous," he says angrily, "that consumers will spend hundreds of bucks for well-designed office chairs and car seats, but nothing on their goddamn commodes!"

The entrepreneur failed once before two years ago with a joint venture that sold brand-name toilet tissue imprinted with issues of *The New York Review of Books*. But this man of ideas doesn't stay inactive long. He has already channeled his energy into a new venture, Tubaquarium, a kit that converts part of the family bathtub into a giant goldfish bowl. "We're getting lots of orders, and our overhead and manufacturing costs are low. I expect to sell a hundred and fifty thousand dollars' worth of the micro-aquariums in the next six months."

LESSONS IN LOSING MEGABUCKS

Part of the trick to becoming an entrepreneur redux is learning how to lose money graciously. The faint of heart who cling to conventional ideas about economic ruination and public disgrace simply can't function in the new entrepreneurial economy. Even the best of guts can mislead the savvy venturer into losing a few million. Some hard-core entretypes don't even take a player seriously unless he or she has lost at least $350,000.

To prepare yourself for the potential of financial ruin associated with the 3.8 failure average, start out small by burning five-dollar bills in your home fireplace. When you've progressed to flinging twenties out your car window, you're on your way to developing the right attitude toward money. The extremely security-minded might want to practice first with Monopoly funds.

Once you're on your way to spectacular failure and spectacular success, you'll need to develop new emotional support strategies to cope with out-of-pocket losses. For some broad guidelines toward the rationalization of financial lapses, consult the following table.

The Sour Grapes Index

Amount You Lost	Rationalizing Remarks
$10,000	A minuscule amount of buying power. Who wants a cheap car, a year's worth of college tuition, or a fairly nice vacation, anyway?
$50,000	So you could have gotten a run-of-the-mill Mercedes, a condominium in Passaic, New Jersey, or a law degree. Who cares?
$300,000	Would just about cover an efficiency loft in Tribeca or a two-bedroom on Nob Hill in San Francisco. Not enough to buy a television station, so what's the big deal?
$1,000,000	Not even enough to buy a diamond ring that would make headlines. Sure, it's nice pocket money, but Johnny Carson makes that much in a month.
$10,000,000	Now we're talking "ouch!" But losing 10 mil isn't totally tragic. You get a big break on your taxes. And think of it this way: If you had been Marlon Brando in 1975 and had turned down a couple of movie offers, you'd have lost about the same amount.

PUTTING A GOOD FACE ON FAILURE

Lazarus types must excel at rationalizing failure not only to themselves, but also to those around them. If you are going to survive setbacks on the road to entrechicdom, you'll have to learn to reinterpret personal failure for an outside audience. What if you're invited to parties at around the time your company is going bankrupt or you've been busted for trying to raise capital by importing heroin? By all means, don't shy away from the company of friends or strangers. Go and have a good time. Chances are you'll be the center of attention, because everyone loves a spectacular failure story as much as they love success sagas. (Maybe even more, because it makes them feel good about their more mundane existences.) Some suggestions for getting the most out of the social scene while embroiled in the process of stupendous failure:

1. Keep your corporate entremobile for classy entrances and exits. When the car goes, so does your entrechic image. If your accountant insists that it be one of the assets liquidated in the disaster, either get another accountant or rent expensive wheels for parties.

2. At social gatherings, never wait for someone to broach the subject of your business humiliations. Launch right into anecdotes that place the blame for your current predicament squarely on all sorts of other bozos, including partners, venture capitalists, secretaries, switchboard operators, business reporters, stockbrokers, the President of the United States, and your parents.

3. Rattle on about your next venture, even if you haven't the vaguest idea what it will be. Make job offers to several party guests. If politically inclined, choose the period following a corporate denouement to announce your intentions to seek a high office and solicit campaign contributions.

THE LONGEVITY OF TYPE E BEHAVIOR

The most entrechic way to success is the fast route, but the entrepreneurial scene also has a place for late bloomers. Because of the many sterling examples of entrechic in these pages, you might be tempted to give up if your enterprise fails to make the *Inc.* 500 in the first six months of operation. But don't despair if it takes you three, five, or fifty years to hit it big on the entrepreneurial scene. By all indications, we are just entering the beginning of what will be many long years devoted to the glorification of self-employment. Moreover, Type E behavior, the obnoxious set of entrepreneurial personality traits that make it impossible for a person to work for anyone else, remains present throughout life, mellowing only slightly with age.

It's Never Too Late: The Hot Senior Ventures of 2035

For those of you who missed the boat during your prime adult years, we offer suggestions for late-life ventures.

NURSING HOME EDITION OF *OLD PEOPLE* MAGAZINE

A great publishing opportunity for the entrepreneurial octogenarian who can put out a slick magazine for a network of nursing home residents. Features could include "Kristy McNichols Talks About Fiber," "Brooke Shields Models the Most Revealing Support Hose," and "How Arnold Schwarzenegger Coped When His Pectorals Hit the Floor."

GEORGE BURNS SEX FRANCHISES

Owners of the franchises will sell a consumer kit including videocassettes of the late, great sex symbol, cigars and eyeglasses, and two inflatable 19-year-old blondes to attach to each arm.

MEMORYJOG SOFTWARE

With this product, no senior consumer need worry about embarassing memory lapses again. Preprograms thousands of names and facts about friends and relatives alive and dead. User-friendly features allow the customer to access information at the flick of a switch.

CODA: BRAVE NEW ENTREWORLD

Those of us in the vanguard of the entrepreneurial movement would like to think that recent developments promise a grand future for seekers of entrechic. The most optimistic observers predict that we are just around the corner from the dawning of an Entrepreneurial Century. Will the megatrends gathering momentum today indeed change the face of our society in the years to come? We decided to look into our entrechic crystal ball. What we saw there verifies our gut feeling that the average citizen's continuing quest for megabucks will deeply affect the American way of life in the next fifteen years.

BEYOND THE MEGA-DECADE: WHAT NEXT?

By the year 2000, the entire country's culture will have changed to make entrepreneurship a mainstream lifestyle for people of all ages. The decentralization process of the Information Age will keep average citizens either at home in front of video monitors or locked in basements and garages starting up enterprises. The major source of information and gossip will be the Gannett newspaper chain's national video news service, *Entrepreneur Today*. Our data also confirm the following major cultural changes.

THE BASICS OF LIFE AT THE DAWN OF THE ENTRECENTURY

FOOD

Entregrazers will dine exclusively on chocolate chip protein cookies and potato-skin-and-broccoli-flavored popcorn. All restaurant entrepreneurs will have converted their facilities to factories manufacturing frozen snack foods for microwave cooking.

SHELTER

Conversion of smokestack factory spaces into living quarters will continue, with an important difference: no longer will citizens be obsessed with natural light. Instead, people will paint windows black to reduce video monitor glare. Underground houses will also become popular.

TRANSPORTATION

Old rusty Mercedes and BMWs will litter the shoulders of abandoned highways. The population will no longer need automobiles, airplanes, or trains, since nobody will leave his or her home/start-up facility. All communication and shopping will take place via personal computer. The biggest status item will be a $35,000 Turbo Saab Modem.

POPULAR CULTURE: TELEVISION

The video revolution of the mid-1980s will lead to substantive lifestyle changes. The average citizen in the year 2000 will watch 15 hours of video programming per day, much of it while in the start-up facility. But instead of enjoying the diversity some communications experts now predict, the television industry will become more narrowly focused on the needs of the entrepreneurial consumer. In 1995, all three major networks will merge to form the EBC (Entrepreneurial Broadcasting Network). Here is what a typical television schedule will look like.

Television Schedule for EBC, December 1, 2000, or 15 A.E. (After Entrechic)

MORNING

6:30 ENTRECISE WITH JOANIE START-UP
Today, Joanie accesses the calf muscles.

7:30 GOOD MORNING, MEGAMERICA!
News and features with hosts Cristina Ferrare and Mitch Kapor.

9:00 THE PETER UEBERROTH SHOW
Hard-hitting interviews with America's most admired go-getter. Today's panel topic: Discrimination against teenage venture capitalists.

10:00 LET'S CUT A DEAL
America's favorite game show with Monty Garage.

10:30 THIS OLD COMPANY
Today, learn how to renovate your human resources department.

11:00 NOTHING VENTURED, NOTHING GAINED
Rollicking new quiz show where contestants risk everything for a shot at mega-millions.

11:30 LEAVE IT TO RONNIE (R) Sitcom
Adorable former President wanders the country, fighting tree pollution and searching for young entrepreneurs in distress. In today's episode, Ronnie visits an Arizona cactus soda magnate about to go broke.

AFTERNOON

12:00 THE "E" TEAM (R)
Battle of Grenada veterans come together to form a special entrepreneurial S.W.A.T force. Today's episode: "I Pity the Fool Who Works Nine to Five."

1:00 THE MICRO-UNITS OF OUR LIVES Soap Opera
Today, Tad learns that Vera slept with Brad in order to get the plans brainstormed by Duncan for the new organic voice synthesizer. Kelly asks Harley for a share of equity in their father's enterprise. Kristen gives birth to test-tube sextuplets and then

attends her company's annual meeting. Garret falls in love with a regularly employed woman and risks his mother's disapproval.

2:00 AFTERNOON MATINEE:
"FlashDeal." (1990) **Teen movie about a nerdy high-schooler who dreams of having his own venture. Popularized the song, "Oh, What a Gut Feeling!"

4:00 VENTURES OF MEGA-MAN
Kiddiepreneur cartoon.

4:30 GENERAL BIRTHING CENTER Soap Opera
Nurse-midwife Kate fights to keep the center out of hierarchical hands. Laurie, a pregnant center director in labor, is kidnapped by extraterrestrials before she can declare her undying love to Lukas, a fellow venturer setting up a nearby deathing center.

5:00 LITTLE BASEMENT ON THE PRAIRIE (R)
Family, circa 1983, battles to carve out a company in a Nebraska basement. Today, Pa rides into town to get a loan for office supplies.

EVENING

6:00 EBC EVENING NEWS
With Anchorman Gary Hart.

7:00 ENTREPRENEURSHIP TONIGHT
Tonight's segments feature the filming of the remake of Francis Ford Coppola's *One From the Heart* and a visit to Mel Gibson's "Downunder" lingerie franchise.

7:30 PEOPLE'S BANKRUPTCY COURT
Judge Wopner presides via video hookup from the Home for Retired TV Father Figures. Tonight, "The Case of the Bogus Business Plan."

8:00 EBC SPECIAL REPORT: HOW GREEN WAS MY SILICON VALLEY?
Investigative report on toxic hazards in the famed entreclave.

10:00 AUSTIN
J.B. threatens to scuttle Bobby Jim's plans for a computer peripherals company unless he forfeits chairmanship of the board. Meanwhile, Miss Elsa reveals that J.B. was not her natural child but a byproduct of an early genetic technology experiment.

11:00 EBC LATE EVENING NEWS
With Donald Trump.

12:00 LATE NIGHT WITH STEVEN JOBS
Steve's guests tonight: Comedian Frank Perdue, Chapstick entrepreneur Julius "Dr. J." Erving, rock musician Steve Wozniak, and Oscar winner Jesse Jackson.

1:30 ROUTE 128 (R)
In 1979, two teenpreneurs set out to seek Massachusetts and megabucks.

2:30 THE LATE SHOW
"Mr. Silicon Chips." (1986) ****Heartwarming classic about a high-tech computer instructor in a small Idaho town.

POLITICS

Our crystal ball shows an amazing political scenario unfolding in the next fifteen years. Some time after a fourth Republican presidential victory puts Jack Kemp in the White House in 1992, a third party composed of disgruntled entrepreneurs and venture capitalists will split off from the Democrats. The Riskocrats will attract a broad constituency including female voters, high-tech types, pushcart owners, and circus performers. Running on a catchy slogan, "An IPO in Every Garage—Let's Make America Mega Again," presidential candidate Lee Iacocca will handily win the 1996 elections, receiving 98.9% of the votes. In fact, his mainstream opponents, David Stockman and Geraldine Ferraro, will concede defeat three months before the general population goes to the polls.

Alas, the reign of the Riskocrats will not be totally free of scandal. A major error in judgment on the part of President Iacocca early in his first term will lead to the Downside Days, when, by presidential decree, anyone owning a Japanese computer or television set will be sent to work in the natural gas fields of Alaska. But the same period will also yield substantial legislative reform, as this short article from *Entrepreneur Today* that appeared in the video receiver of our crystal ball attests:

ERA Signed By President Today

(Entrewire Services) President Iacocca today signed the Entrepreneurial Rights Act (ERA). The bill guarantees every citizen the right to $500,000 in start-up capital for two enterprises and allows spouses to transfer their capitalization stipends to one another. The money will come out of a fund started by megamillionaires who found they still had plenty of spare cash after helping to pay off the national deficit last year. "This is an upside day for America," said the nation's First Entrepreneur. Vice President Robert Noyce was also present, as was Cabinet member Jane Fonda, Secretary of Video Production.

THE LANGUAGE

One of the surest indications of social norms is language. Looking into the future has enabled us to see how the new entrepreneurial emphasis will become reflected in idioms and new constructions that will become popular between now and the year 2000. Each time we gaze into the crystal ball, we notice several phrases that keep popping up again and again. For example, "Gawd, work me nine to five!" seems to be the post-entrechic equivalent of the early 1980s expression, "Gag me with a spoon!"

Words now esoteric or obsolete will be reclaimed and rehabilitated to add to the entrepreneurial vocabulary. In fact, the incredible number of new vocabulary terms indicates that the America of the twenty-first century will be a civilization obsessed by the entrechic lifestyle. Since the majority of the words we encountered in the crystal ball are currently obsolete terms accessible only in the *Oxford English Dictionary*, we suspect a premeditated infusion of new terms into the language, perhaps under direct orders of the Riskocratic government. Here are some examples of the peculiar vocabulary that will develop in the next decade and a half.

Entr'acte. Meaning in 1985: interval between two successive acts of a theatrical performance, *or* an entertainment provided during this interval. Meaning in 2000: An actor who produces his own movies.

Entraverse. In 1450: rare adjective meaning *crosswise*. In 2000: all planets containing viable entrepreneurial activity.

Entrechat. In 1985: a leap in ballet during which the dancer crosses his feet a number of times, often beating them together. In 2000: a friendly networking conversation.

Entrecote. In 1985: a specific cut of steak from between the ribs. In 2000: a corduroy sports jacket.

Entrecounter. In 1550: to set oneself in opposition. In 2000: meeting between one or more mega-millionaires under the age of 35.

Entregent. In 1650: rare word meaning *social intercourse*. In 2000: British businessman.

Entremedley. In 1430: adjective meaning *intermixed*. In 2000: a Muzak arrangement designed for nonhierarchical workplaces.

Entremess. In 1700: a dish served between the main courses. In 2000: cafeteria for skunkworks.

Entrepot. In 1985: temporary storage depot. In 2000: marijuana grown in garages.

Entrepraignant. In 1475: rare adjective meaning *enterprising*. In 2000: adjective describing single woman who chooses to start up a pregnancy.

Entrepressed. In 1641: pressed between two objects. In 2000: clothes dry-cleaned by an entrepreneurial method.

Entreproche. In 1475: to approach one another. In 2000: an innovative acquisition strategy.

Entresalue. In 1490: to greet one another. In 2000: traditional toast at start-up parties; slang for *hello* and *goodbye*.

Entresigns. In 1480: sign or token, *especially* sign on knight's armor. In 2000: sociological truths, also known as megatrends.

Entresol. In 1985: mezzanine. In 2000: a type of fish favored for deal-cutting luncheons.

Entropium. In 1870: inversion of the eyelids. In 2000: venture-related burnout.

THE CONCEPT OF A BRIGHT AND HAPPY MEGA-FUTURE

By looking fifteen years into the future, we now know that the current entrepreneurial climate is but an incubator for a more glorious age to come. Indeed, a short ten years after the entrepreneurial decade is slated to end, we will enter an entrepreneurial century full of innovation. All would-be entrepreneurs can look forward to a time when mankind will finally be free of time-based shackles and able to explore his true inner-direction. But the knowledge that even better times are yet to come for risk-taking innovators should not make us complacent. Only those who have a few start-ups and sell-outs under their belts will be in a position to reap the maximum megabucks at the dawn of the coming entrecentury.

Once you enter the world of entrechic, you face a window of opportunity into a promised land where anything is possible. Don't just look toward the window: brainstorm through it. Entrepreneuring is risky business, but it's worth it. Remember, the unerring pursuit of entrechic means more than just money. If you hit the right concept, it could even mean access to immortality. Risk it!